Clergy Under Stress

Clergy Under Stress

*A study of homosexual and heterosexual
clergy in the Church of England*

Dr Ben (C.) Fletcher

MOWBRAY

Mowbray
A Cassell imprint
Villiers House, 41/47 Strand, London WC2N 5JE, England

First published 1990

British Library Cataloguing in Publication Data
Fletcher, Ben (C.)
    Clergy under stress.
    1. Church of England. Homosexual clergy
    I. Title
    262. 1434208664

ISBN 0-264-67196-1

Typeset by Area Graphics Ltd
Printed and bound in Great Britain by Biddles Ltd, Guildford and King's Lynn

Contents

Foreword

Dr Jack Dominian

We are living at a time when there is a great deal of interest in God, and much disillusionment with the institutional Churches. The responsibility for providing a continuous parochial presence in this atmosphere of indifference is largely in the hands of the clergy who every week provide regular services throughout Britain. The Church of England is largely responsible for the spiritual welfare of the country, and some 10,000 of its clergy have the demanding task of leading in worship and ensuring that the manifold needs of people are met. Numbers attending services are few, demands heavy, and when things go wrong criticism is rampant. All this adds up to one word, stress.

The psychological sciences have been studying stress for several decades, and there is little doubt that it is a killer. There is evidence that some of the commonest lethal diseases, such as heart disease and cancer of all types, are adversely affected by stress, which can both initiate these conditions and aggravate them when they are established.

It is pertinent, therefore, to know what degree of stress the clergy of the Church of England are subject to. Dr Ben Fletcher has undertaken an in-depth study of their problem, which reveals in considerable detail some of the answers. The analysis of the material is not easy reading, but it deserves the greatest attention and perseverance, for his range of enquiry is wide and deep, and touches many aspects of clerical life.

The conclusions are that, while the vast majority of the clergy experience some stress, this is not high, and I think the country owes an enormous debt of gratitude to the dedication and commitment of these men who are battling to preserve Christianity in a poor Christian era.

Whilst the majority of clergy are able to function reasonably well, there is a small but sizeable minority who exhibit a great deal of stress. These are the clergy with a homosexual orientation. Their problems are extensive and are studied in depth in this book.

From my own experience the difficulties of homosexual clergy are not confined to the Church of England, and in this respect the book can be read with advantage by the Roman Catholic Church, whose rule of celibacy attracts a fair number of homosexuals offering themselves for the priesthood.

There are many factors that contribute to stress, but above all we all need a unity in which the inner and the outer person can function in an integrated way. For many homosexuals this tolerance is lacking in their life and they have to live double lives at a considerable price.

The problem of homosexuality faces all denominations, and I hope this study brings the day nearer when Christianity can come to conclusions about this subject which will allow homosexual men and women to be honest about their orientation, and serve the Church without the enormous pain they currently endure.

The author of this book started with no prejudices or assumptions in his study of the Church of England clergy. His findings are not only fascinating for their intrinsic scientific worth, but because they shed light in an area where too little is available.

He deserves our congratulations and gratitude, and I hope that his findings will spread widely and lead to the necessary changes so that clergy can continue their dedicated task with the minimum of stress in their lives.

Preface

The writing of this book has been a salutary experience for me. Before I started the research presented here I knew little about the Church of England, even less about homosexuals, and nothing about homosexual clergy. I have learned a lot. I thank all the clergy who provided the data, but particularly the homosexual clergy for their openness and courage, and for the trust they showed in me. I hope all clergy will find the book reflects their true perceptions of the situations they are in. My impartiality has probably meant that I have ignored aspects of the human side of the suffering encapsulated in the figures. I would specifically like to thank the priest who provided the case study in Chapter 5.

The book is concerned with stress among Church of England clergy, although, owing to the results obtained from two large surveys, later chapters concentrate on the position of homosexual clergy. Chapter 1 provides an introduction to some of the scientific literature showing that psychological factors affect physical health. Chapter 2 presents a study of stress among parochial clergy. Chapters 3-5 present evidence showing that homosexual clergy are suffering very high levels of stress and disillusionment with the Church. The research probably represents the first scientific attempt to estimate the extent of the problem and the causes of strain among the clergy.

Chapter 6 contains a recent history of some of the General Synod and other debates on the issue of homosexuality in the Church and outlines some ways in which the Church of England could begin to alleviate the serious problems it is faced with in this respect.

The book was written to appeal to all clergy and any interested in the topic of stress in a more general way. Because of the sensitive nature of some of the subject-matter, and the controversial issues covered, I have erred marginally on the side of science rather than easy reading: as a result some very simple statistics are reported for the more numerate reader. Those wishing to have more detailed and sophisticated analyses of the data presented here should contact me at Hatfield Polytechnic.

Overall, the Church of England is not shown to be as caring of its employees as I had imagined beforehand. The Church appears to be worried about tackling some of the difficult issues partly from a genuine concern over how the public would view it, but also partly because of the power of some political groupings within it. This needs to change for the good of the Church and the good of the clergy.

This book is dedicated to my wife, Dr Anita Jackson.

Dr Ben (C.) Fletcher
St Albans, November 1989

1

Stress and Health

Stress can kill. It is responsible for more industrial disease than any other aspect of work. It compromises the immune system, plays a highly important role in the onset of major diseases, and can result in premature death. It also makes people feel anxious and depressed, lowers their job and life satisfaction, makes for bad decisions and poor organisational climate, increases alcohol and cigarette consumption, increases health service costs, leads to accidents, and reduces efficiency. These aspects are only the tip of the iceberg. What is so strange is that employers and governments are largely ignoring the problem and even worry about addressing the issue of stress in case it raises expectations that something will be done about it or, even worse, that the very mention of the word causes people to think about the issues. Many people are aware of stress but are ignorant of the costs involved, many deny it is a problem, and many do not think that anything can be done about it anyway. This is rather like not going to the doctor about the lump on the breast or the chest pains. These things may go away, but they also may not. Ignoring such issues makes no sense – even if it is found that nothing is wrong. In the same way as it makes sense to have medical check-ups, it makes sense for people and organisations to have stress audits regularly.

This book is about stress in the Church of England. In particular, it presents two studies I have made to investigate the extent of stress problems among the clergy. The first study looks at parochial clergy and the second concentrates on a special group of clergy – homosexual priests. The purpose of these studies is to examine what aspects of work and other factors may be responsible for the levels of stress observed.

They are also attempts, perhaps for the first time, to estimate objectively the extent of the stress problems in the Church of England. Most of the previous research on stress in ministers of religion has been conducted in countries other than the UK, and none, to my knowledge, has systematically investigated the position of homosexual clergy. Before outlining these studies, however, it is necessary to introduce some of the concepts central to the work, and some of the previous research showing how important stress may be.

Stressors and strains

Stress is a difficult word giving rise to many woolly interpretations. For this reason it is necessary to distinguish between 'stressors' and 'strains'. Stressors are environmental or psychosocial factors which cause the individual to suffer strain. Strain is the consequence of being exposed to stressors of sufficient magnitude or duration. Stressors are the precursors or causes of strain. Strain may be manifested in many ways, including psychological ill-health and elevation of biological risk factors (such as blood pressure, hormonal changes, immune deficiency). Stressors may be major enough to have a relatively immediate and observable effect on a person (the death of a close friend, or changing jobs, for example). They may, however, be less obvious to the person affected and even go unnoticed. Stressors may not even be considered to be harmful by the person exposed to them. This is why stress is so often considered a 'silent killer': stressors which persist for some length of time may have a cumulative and insidious effect on the person's well-being. It is important to distinguish between stressors as activators, and strains as reactions to them: between causes and consequences.

Stress and the immune system

There may be readers who consider that stress is not an explanatory concept at all, but just a rag-bag for all the as yet unexplained physical or medical causes of psychological and organic disturbances which are the basis of illness. Such an attitude is naive and does not do justice to the necessary interrelationship between the mind and the body. Psychological and medical sciences go hand in hand and each needs the other to explain how and why body and mind break down from time to time. Why is it, for example, that for many viral invasions of the body such as colds and flu only a small proportion of those infected develop the clinical symptoms? Why are there personality differences in susceptibility? It is now recognised that the immune system and the cardiovascular system are conditionable (that is, they learn) and must be considered as integral *behavioural* systems. This can be illustrated by an example. In one study,[1] some rats were given a drink of sodium saccharin at the same time as they were injected with a powerful immune system suppressant. After a further three days some of the animals were given a second drink of the sodium saccharin. This second drink was found to have a powerful immunosuppressive effect by itself, as a consequence of once previously having been given at the same time as a biological immunosuppressive: the immune system had learned. Given that humans are probably much more susceptible than rats to psychological influences, one can only ponder the learning effects that might affect the immune system. Studies on humans have shown that bereavement, long vigils, surgery, examination taking and loneliness can all have a marked effect on immune system functioning. For example, students who are lonely have poorer immune-system responses than those who are not, and separated or divorced women have fewer natural killer cells (implicated in cancer surveillance) than married controls and the more emotionally attached they were to their husbands the less their immune system is able to fight infections.[2]

One particularly interesting demonstration of the powerful effect of psychological factors on immune functioning is given by Smith and MacDaniel.[3] They gave students the TB scratch test once a month for six months on one arm and a saline scratch on the other. The TB scratch test is given to ascertain whether or not a person already has the antibodies in his blood to fight tuberculin infection. If he has, a red lump, the Mantoux reaction, develops at the site of the TB scratch. Nothing develops where the saline scratch is given. The investigators only used students who showed this delayed reaction. However, in the sixth month, some students, without being told in advance, were given the TB and saline scratches on different arms to those they were expecting to be tested on. What the researchers found was that expectancy had a very significant effect on the size of the Mantoux lump that resulted: it was much smaller than normal because the students were expecting it to appear on the other arm. If such simple psychological factors as expectancy can so affect such a basic biological process, imagine what could happen with more powerful ones.

The mechanisms for this interplay between the mind and the body are only just beginning to be understood. For example, there have been demonstrations that the anti-anxiety drugs known as benzodiazepines, which include Valium, are themselves very potent stimulators of immune defence, and it seems that white blood cells, one type of the immune-system cells, have brain hormone receptors for a substance called ACTH which is produced in the brain's pituitary gland and inhibits the production of antibodies. This implies that the brain and the immune system speak the same language and are constantly in intimate dialogue.

It is no longer in dispute that psychological stressors affect the body's ability to fight disease.

Stress and heart disease

Coronary heart disease (CHD) is a generic term which is used to describe both coronary atherosclerosis (or clogged-up arteries) and myocardial infarction (heart attack). Such diseases are responsible for the deaths of nearly half of all men of working age, and over one-quarter of all women of working age. There is a vast amount of research showing that psychological factors act as stressors affecting the cardio-vascular system. For example, in coronary patients it has been shown that mental stress in the form of public speaking, reading, doing maths and other cognitive tasks can produce abnormalities in the heart wall, without any accompanying chest pain, as great in magnitude as that caused by treadmill exercise.[4]

One factor which has received considerable investigation is person-ality. The view that personality factors play a significant role in the development of heart disease was pioneered by two investigators in the USA, Friedman and Rosenman. They coined the phrase 'Type A' or 'coronary-prone behaviour' characterised by: extreme competitive-ness; constant striving for achievement; high job involvement; aggres-siveness and hostility in interactions; haste; impatience; explosiveness of speech; tense facial expression; feeling of being under pressure of time and high responsibility; constantly having to do more and more.

Around 50 per cent of people would be categorised as Type As, with half of them showing it in more extreme forms. Type Bs are those who have an absence of Type A characteristics. Type A behaviour has been associated with an increased risk of heart disease. In a follow-up study of over 3,000 men initially free of coronary heart disease, Type A men aged 39–49 years old were 6.5 times more likely to have developed CHD within two and a half years than their counterpart Type B personalities. In later follow-ups the magnitude of the difference has reduced, but even when all traditional risk factors for heart disease, such as parental history of heart disease, blood pressure, cholesterol and triglyceride levels, have been controlled, the overall excess risk of being Type A was about twofold (although a 22-year follow-up suggests the risk may have disappeared by then[5]). In studies which have measured both biological and psychosocial variables, such as personality and religious affiliations, the psychosocial variables are at least as good as the biological variables in predicting heart disease, and usually better.

Why do Type A people seem to be 'coronary-prone'? There are a number of possible reasons. First, they are likely to take on more work and overload themselves, which is itself a risk factor. Second, Type As do not appear to have a well-developed self-awareness of what is happening to them. On a treadmill, they will do more physical work than Type Bs and will not admit to being as fatigued: they do not seem to suffer from subjective distress as easily and are more prone to use the unconscious coping strategies of denial and suppression. It has also been suggested that they are more likely to cope consciously with the situation. Type A individuals also seem to have a more labile or reactive physiological system: in the same situation their body will react more by showing greater arousal and hormone excretion. For example, David Glass from New York has shown that under competitive game-playing conditions, Type As show greater blood pressure changes and higher levels of adrenalin excretion than Type Bs when they are playing with a harassing opponent, although no differences are observed under normal playing conditions. It also seems that Type A individuals show enhanced reactions physiologically when they cannot control the situation they are in. Finally, it appears that whatever is the basis for the differences reported above, it is not the case that Type A differences are a result of conscious strategies which affect the body. In a study of patients during surgery,[6] Type A people show greater blood pressure changes during coronary bypass surgery when they are anaesthetised (as much as 30 mmHg higher than Type Bs) and are more likely to have complications during the operation which are due to sympathetic nervous system activity. To comfort Type A individuals, it is worth pointing out that Type As are better at surviving heart attacks than Type Bs: if they survive the following twenty-four hours the death rate is some 42 per cent lower.[7]

Recent research suggests that the effects of personality on CHD is more complicated than previously thought. It seems that other negative emotions are also likely to play a role. In a review paper published recently, the authors concluded that: 'Overall the picture of the coronary-prone personality emerging... seems to be one of a person with one or more negative emotions: perhaps someone who is depressed, aggressively competitive, easily frustrated, anxious, angry or some combination.'[8]

Personality is not the only factor of psychological relevance related to coronary heart disease risk. Social factors are important too. The social environment in which the person lives can have a marked effect on resistance to disease. Meaningful, and therefore relatively long-term, social contacts act as social supports and can have a protective effect. For example, the particularly strong patriarchal Catholic Italian-Americans of Roseta in Pennsylvania, who have a very cohesive and strong social structure with clearly defined social roles, were shown to have less than half the rate of heart attacks than a nearby town which was socially heterogeneous. In a study of the effects of social networks in Alameda County, California, Berkman and Syme[9] have shown that those with few social ties were over twice as likely to have died from heart disease and cancer as those with more extensive networks. Marriage, it seems, also has a protective effect. Being geographically mobile, and making many job moves, however, causes a disruption of social networks and a doubling of heart disease risk. It has also been argued that the higher rates of heart disease apparent in lower income groups in the UK may also be partly associated with a low degree of social support.[10] I have also argued that concordance in the heart disease mortality risks of marital partners, which show an occupationally specific effect, are due to occupational stressors being transmitted between husband and wife.[11]

Stress and cancer

Cancer is the leading cause of death in women of working age in England and Wales, and kills over a quarter of men under 65 years old. In recent years there has been a remarkable growth in the weight of scientific evidence suggesting that stress plays a causal role in cancer. Physical environmental agents do not provide either necessary or sufficient causes of cancer. For example, only about 10 per cent of heavy smokers die of lung cancer, and 10 per cent of lung cancer sufferers have never smoked.

Evidence that stress plays a role in cancer includes a considerable amount of animal research showing that quite mild stressors can affect tumour development and growth. The range of stressors include such things as rotating the animals, small electric shocks, handling them when young, varying cage-population density, or socially isolating them. It seems that the more unpredictable the stressor, or the less control the animal can exercise over it, the greater the tumour growth. Stress hormones, such as corticosterone, can also produce a marked enhancement of tumour growth.

The human evidence is increasingly strong. For example, one large study[12] suggests that students who subsequently went on to develop cancers, especially the major ones, later in life perceived themselves as less close to their parents. Father–son relationships demonstrated the strongest links with cancer. It also seems that feelings of hopelessness and depression may be related to cancer risk. In the late 1960s two investigators, Schmale and Iker,[13] did a psychological investigation of women attending a hospital after having positive cervical smears. They were given cone biopsies to determine whether the abnormalities were cancerous or not, but prior to the outcome of the biopsies were classified according to the degree to which they exhibited feelings of hopelessness in response to life events that had occurred in the preceding six months. From this information alone the researchers were able to categorise correctly over 75 per cent of the women in terms of whether or not they had malignant cells present. More recently, investigating women with breast cancer, research has shown that recurrence-free survival after five years may be significantly lower in women who respond to their diagnosis with feelings of stoic acceptance or hopelessness of their situation, compared to those who exhibited a fighting spirit or a denial of their cancer.[14]

Other aspects of personality have also been linked to cancer risk. Two cancer-prone personality characteristics are:

1. Repression of emotions, rational or non-emotional reactions or remaining distant and isolated from emotionally important objects such as people.

2. Ambivalent or inconsistent reactions to situations, such as having different feelings or behaving in a different way to the same situation on different occasions.

Professor Hans Eysenck, in a review in the *British Journal of Medical Psychology,* reports one large study in which the score on a rational–anti-emotional scale was eight times more predictive of lung cancer risk than smoking behaviour.[15]

Cancer rates are also affected by social factors. It seems, for example, that married people have lower overall mortality rates for cancer, compared to those who are not married, and that the unmarried also have lower survival rates, are more likely to be untreated for the cancer, and are more likely to present for diagnosis when their cancer is at a more regional or distant stage, rather than locally confined.[16]

Work stress and health

I have shown elsewhere[17] that work stressors are likely to be a major factor in determining the life expectancy and cause of death of those in the work environment and those who interact with them. It seems likely that occupational stressors can be transmitted through psychological mechanisms to affect the disease risks of both partners in a marriage. In many ways this is not surprising if you begin to contemplate the many and subtle ways in which work affects how you think and behave, although the very specific occupational risks on both partners I reported were remarkable: for example, machine tool setters and their wives have different life expectancies and causes of death from machine tool operators.

What work stressors influence health and well-being is the subject of this brief section. There are likely to be many different stressors in any work environment. For example, in a national survey conducted by one of my PhD students, Frederick Stone, we found 129 different stressors which were associated with increased depression and anxiety. In that survey, 49 per cent of the sample reported that much of their work occurred in bursts, all or most of the time, and the more this happened the higher the strain levels. Some 24 per cent reported poor management, 24 per cent poor communications, 28 per cent poor workplace layouts, 27 per cent too many working hours, 20 per cent that they were usually dealing with conflicting demands, 31 per cent that their capabilities were not sufficiently used, and 35 per cent felt they had no career prospects. The purpose of models is to rationalise them into meaningful units to make explanatory sense. If this were not done it would be very difficult indeed to compare jobs in terms of stress profiles. Two models of occupational stress will be outlined which provide a backcloth to the two empirical studies of clergy stress described in detail in later chapters. Both these models are useful in predicting why it is that, in general, the higher up the occupational ladder one goes the lower the levels of strain.[18] Stress is clearly not to be equated with the degree of demand individuals are subjected to.

The first model was developed by Professor Peter Warr[19] and is known as the Vitamin Model. This model suggests that the biological analogy of the vitamin requirements of the body is useful for understanding why occupational stressors produce strain. It proposes that the work environment must provide the person with a balance of nine different vitamins. If it fails to do this, and the situation persists, ill-health will result. A minimum amount of each vitamin is necessary for proper functioning, although beyond a certain level of intake the vitamins are not beneficial. Some vitamins such as A and D, however, can produce toxic effects if they are taken in large quantities and these are called the additional decrement vitamins – too much of a good thing. Constant-effect vitamins, on the other hand, such as C and E, are not toxic in large doses and, while above a certain level they fail to do any more good, they do no harm either. Table 1.1 shows the nine aspects of work Warr believes affect health. A job will produce strain, according to this view, if it does not supply adequate amounts of the vitamins, if the intake is out of balance, or if it gives the person an excess of the additional decrement stressors.

Table 1.1 Warr's Nine Occupational Stress Vitamins

The constant-effect or CE vitamins

1. Financial remuneration
2. Physical working conditions (adequacy)
3. Social position of the job

The additional decrement or AD vitamins

4. Degree of job control, discretion or autonomy
5. Degree of skill required by the job
6. Amount of variety in the work
7. The work demands or goals
8. How clearly defined the job is
9. The amount of social interaction required

The second model, which Professor Roy Payne and I have developed, forms the basis of one of the most up-to-date measures of occupational stressors and strains, my own Cultural Audit or Occupational Stress Audit.[20] The model proposes that strain is the result of the lack of balance between three work factors:

Job demands. This is the degree to which the work environment contains stimuli which peremptorily require attention and response. The stimuli might be technical, intellectual, social, financial. Job demands are the things that have to be done and the environment in which the individual is placed. Table 1.2 presents some common job demands.

Job supports. This is the degree to which the work environment contains available resources which are relevant to the demands of the individual or the group. These supports may be technical, intellectual, social, financial, etc. For example, being part of a happy cohesive workforce may make the job demands easier to cope with.

Job constraints. Jobs are made much harder by the lack of relevant resources. Such constraints can act to prevent the individual from maximising the benefits of the supports, as well as affect how they can cope with the demands. Thus constraints are those aspects of the working environment which prevent the worker or group from coping with the demands. Table 1.2 shows some common support–constraints (for operational reasons, supports and constraints are treated as a single dimension).

Table 1.2 Work stressors as demands or supports–constraints

Work demands	Work supports–constraints
Job pressure	Being clear about role
Having too much to do	Job discretion, autonomy or control
Having too little to do	Quality of relationships with:
Being responsible	Boss
for people	Colleagues
Responsibility for things	Subordinates
(equipment)	Union membership
Demands from others	Role ambiguity
Conflicting demands/roles	Variety level/skill utilisation
Over/under-promotion	Social perception of job
Keeping up with others/	Participation in decisions
organisations	Payment/reward system
Organisational climate	Quality of equipment
Office politics	Physical working conditions
Organisational structure	How work is planned/managed
Organisational/job	
changes	
Major decisions	
Expectancies of others/	
organisation	

According to the Demands–Support–Constraints model of stress, strain results from a lack of balance between the three variables. Thus high job demands are not stressful if the job also provides good levels of support and low constraints. In fact, high demands can be positively good in the right circumstances because they provide stimulation and utilise the workers' abilities – underutilisation of abilities and boredom are among the most potent stressors and also usually occur in work environments where supports are low and constraints high. One obvious practical implication of the model is that highly demanding jobs can be made less stressful without reducing the level of the demands: instead, the level of supports can be increased or the constraints reduced. The model has implications for redesigning work to reduce the amount of strain in an organisation while at the same time boosting efficiency.

This model has been tested on a whole array of occupational groups (managers, teachers, nurses, taxi drivers, students, lorry drivers) and certainly has predictive value. It is important to note, however, that the central concept of support does not simply refer to social or interpersonal aspects, although these are known to reduce the effects of stress.

It also includes such job factors as being clear about the task in hand and having a measure of autonomy and discretion over how the work is ordered and executed. These aspects have been shown to have very important consequences for health, too. For example, Professor Robert Karasek has done a considerable amount of work to show that job discretion can moderate the effects of job demands on the cardiovascular system. In situations of high demand, blood adrenalin levels are increased, with consequent changes in blood pressure and blood lipid values. It seems, however, that low discretion or lack of control is also associated with higher levels of the stress hormone cortisol. Karasek suggests that the worst combination for the cardiovascular system is when demands are high and are not offset by controllability. He has applied this to the long-term prediction of heart disease rates in both the USA and Sweden.[21] It was found that having low job discretion significantly increased the risk of heart attacks, over and above the effects of job demands. In another study it was found that the job characteristics which discriminated the high from the low heart disease-risk jobs were those which showed low control or discretion accompanied by a rushed work tempo. This relationship between job demands and job discretion has also been successful in predicting pill consumption, depression rates, feelings of exhaustion, absence from work, life and job satisfaction.[22]

Both the studies reported in this book included measures of job demands and job supports–constraints which can be used to determine if both affect the amount of strain clergy experience as a consequence of their work. Chapter 2 will outline the first study of stress among parochial clergy, after a consideration of the previous research that has been done on stress in ministers of religion.

Notes

1. Ader and Cohen, 1985.
2. Kiecolt-Glaser *et al.*, 1987.
3. Smith and MacDaniel, 1983.
4. Rozanski *et al.*, 1988.
5. Ragland and Brand, 1988a.
6. Krantz *et al.*, 1982.
7. Ragland and Brand, 1988b.
8. Booth-Kewley and Friedman, 1987.
9. Berkman and Syme, 1979.
10. See Fletcher, 1988a.
11. Fletcher, 1988b.
12. The study was done by Thomas and her associates. An example of the research findings can be found in Thomas, Duszynski and Shaffer, 1979.
13. See, for example, Schmale and Iker, 1966.
14. Greer, Morris and Pettingdale, 1979.
15. Eysenck, 1988.
16. Goodwin *et al.*, 1987.
17. Fletcher, 1988b.
18. See Fletcher and Payne, 1980a, 1980b; Fletcher, 1988b.
19. Warr, 1987.
20. Fletcher, 1990.
21. Karasek, Russell *et al.*, 1982; Karasek, Theorell *et al.*, 1982.
22. Karasek, 1979.

2

Stress among Parochial Clergy

In Chapter 1 a number of potential stressors were outlined which have been implicated in work-related strain. Of course, the number of possible stressors is almost infinite and will depend to some extent on the actual job being investigated, or the context in which the work is done. None the less many general work stressors have been identified. Being a Church of England cleric, however, does have its own particular hazards and it is these which I will address next. This chapter will detail some of the earlier research on stress among ministers of religion. Since nearly all the relevant research has been done in other countries, the chapter will concentrate on reporting the results of a project recently completed by the Reverend David MacPherson and myself on Church of England parochial clergy.[1]

Previous studies of stress among ministers of religion

There is conflicting evidence from research in other countries on the question of whether ministers of religion suffer from high levels of job stress. In a PhD thesis done at the Fuller Theological Seminary in Pasadena, USA, Blackmon[2] in 1984 shows evidence from studies which suggest that three-quarters of all clergy have suffered major stress and one-third have had serious thought about leaving their vocation. MacDonald[3] reports that clergy who are particularly likely to quit their vocation are those between 30 and 49 years old (mid-life crisis?), those with small parishes and those with a liberal theology. The literature which most supports the view that clergy might suffer high levels of stress is in the area of 'Burnout', and Richmond, Rayburn and Rogers[4] suggest that it is very common among clergy. Burnout is akin to emotional exhaustion[5] and has many similarities with the symptoms of depression. It is particularly relevant to clergy because it has been identified as a problem which results from the effects of interpersonal demands in the caregiving professions, including the clergy.[6] Burnout results from people distancing themselves from their 'clients'. As a consequence they appear less concerned and involved; they may experience physical and psychological fatigue, alienation and feelings of failure. In addition, burnout has been associated with headaches, gastrointestinal problems, weight loss, inability to sleep, shortness of breath, mood swings, lack of tolerance, suspiciousness, cynicism, risk-taking, negative attitudes, inability to relax, substance abuse, and poor socialising.[7] Burnout may also have a spiritual dimension relevant to clergy since it can result in a loss of idealism as well as energy. It occurs particularly in those who are 'motivated by idealistic values of service and professional goals, in addition to the usual reasons for work'.[8]

Stress probably plays an important causal role in burnout. Doohan lists the causes as

conflict between needs and accomplishment, unrealistic dedication, use of work as a substitute for a satisfying personal life, an authoritarian management style, and an inability to delegate authority and say no to unreasonable demands... a lack of talent or ability to achieve a goal, inadequate education or training, overidentification with those served, and an inability to communicate strong feelings.[9]

Given that stress may play a role in burnout it is important to know how stressful the jobs of clergy really are. Unfortunately, a great deal of the research on burnout is too poorly quantified and inadequately controlled to make scientifically useful statements. Although clergy appear to be in a profession which could be susceptible to burnout, are they really at risk? Daniel and Rogers[10] suggest four particular reasons why they are:

1. Individuals who take up the ministry are not sufficiently aware of their limits, nor of their motivation for entering the profession.

2. The personality profiles of those who enter the Church make them susceptible to burnout. They quote a review of 38 studies with clergy or prospective clergy using a well-established personality test (the MMPI) which showed: 'The consistency of the MMPI profiles

obtained from the religious samples is most striking.... This pattern suggests that the religious tend to be more perfectionist, worrisome, introversive, socially inept and in more extreme cases, perhaps isolated and withdrawn.'[11]

3. The Church does not provide in-service training or graduate training in dealing with interpersonal stress or the interpersonal processes which provide the cleric with realistic goals and good self-understanding. Problems can arise if the individual cannot grasp the difference between dispositional problems and those which are a consequence of the situation.

4. At the organisational level the Church does not provide adequate support and advice, and there is little opportunity for group-based work on a regular basis. Moreover, in the words of Lauer the Church could be accused of 'structured punishment' of clergy because 'Churches expect their ministers to do the impossible. His primary calling is spiritual, says the layman, but the minister is judged on organisational rather than spiritual criteria. The minister is a social being but tends not to have meaningful relationships with church members. The minister should not worry about money yet salary schedules may be inadequate.'[12]

Lauer reports an interview study of 25 Protestant Church ministers and 252 Church members from a metropolitan area in the USA. Sixty-one per cent of the members and 64 per cent of the ministers considered that the job of the minister was more stressful than the job of the lay members. In addition only 14 per cent of members and 0 per cent of ministers felt the members' jobs were more stressful. Lauer suggests that this stress arises because 'Both the minister and his members are caught up in a network of expectations that are inevitably thwarted':[13] for example, the minister is expected to be an exemplary Christian whose primary role is a man of God (69 per cent of members) while at the same time he has great importance as an administrator (rated very important by 82 per cent of members). Lauer also reports that ministers reported many fewer leisure hours than members (for example, 10.6 hours a week as against 24.9) and the difficulties of not having sufficient time to do their work were also reflected in the fact that lack of time was ranked the number one problem. One minister, for example, said:

You feel like your work is with you all the time. There is always a mountain of work ahead and many things you know that should be done and you can't get to them. It requires a lot of vigour and health to keep going; and if this ebbs, your mountain of work looks even larger and so you feel that you are never done.[14]

A study of 189 Presbyterians by Warner and Carter[15] compared the stress of being a pastor (or pastor's wife) with that experienced by lay members of the denomination. The authors measured loneliness, marital adjustment and four aspects of burnout from the Maslach Burnout Inventory: emotional exhaustion, personal accomplishment, depersonalisation and involvement. The pastors and pastors' wives came out in a significantly worse position than their respective lay control groups: they were more lonely and showed less adjustment to their marital situation. Moreover, pastors' wives experienced more emotional exhaustion, and pastors more involvement than their control groups. Warner and Carter interpret the findings as indicating that owing to the considerable role demands faced by pastors they have to become heavily involved in their job. As a consequence, extra burdens are placed on the wife, leading to emotional exhaustion. Both these aspects lead to withdrawal, causing loneliness and less marital satisfaction.

Precisely what work stressors clergy may be exposed to has been investigated in a study of New Zealand ministers of religion by Dewe.[16] All ordained members of the Protestant Church were sent questionnaires which asked about 48 different sources of work stress and 65 possible ways of coping with the demands. The items included in the questionnaire were derived from interviews with a sample of 38 ministers. Dewe reports an excellent response rate of 60 per cent from the clergy. Most of the respondents were male (92 per cent), most were married (90 per cent), most did parish work (82 per cent), with an average age of 46 years, 16 years in the ministry and an average of three appointments.

The clergy were asked how frequently the work stressors occurred and how often they used each of the coping strategies, on a 5-point scale. A principal components analysis was performed on these responses (which is a way of distilling the data in a manner to produce a smaller descriptive set of factors). The work stressors revealed three factors:

1. *Parish conflicts and church conservatism* (the best predictor of the frequency with which clergy experienced the stress). The items which were the primary determinants of this factor included:
   Conflict between the traditionally expected style of ministry and the way you see yourself using your skills and your gifts.
   Other people not accepting you for what you are.

Church conservatism – the conflict between tradition and change.

People not realising that a minister also needs support.

The feeling that people forget that ministers are like anyone else – they too have needs and desires.

The feeling that you are continually propping up a cumbersome institutional structure.

The feeling that society expects you to be able to help with all problems at all times.

Being asked to make statements on questions you have not yet personally resolved.

2. *Difficulties involving parish commitment and development* for which the primary items included:

The lack of commitment from parishioners.

The reluctance to grow.

Meeting apathy.

The feeling of inadequacy because not meeting the full pastoral needs of people.

Lack of training in certain fields.

Inadequacy of parish finance.

3. *Emotional and time difficulties involving crisis work:* which centred on such aspects as:

Dealing with others' marital problems.

Conflict between planned and crisis work.

Too much to do in the time available.

Dealing with people in desperate need.

Dealing with funerals.

Necessary and important tasks being overshadowed because of the number of administrative duties to be carried out.

The analysis of the coping strategies revealed five factors, and it will be noticed that the vast majority can be described as palliative rather than problem-solving or direct-action strategies:

1. *Social support* (the most important factor) which included such items as:

Talk about the situation with someone else.

Try to get advice and suggestions from someone else.

Express your irritation to other colleagues to be able to let off steam.

Draw on colleagues to develop your own skills and beliefs.

2. *Postponing action by relaxing and distracting attention,* which included:
> Drop what you are doing and take up something totally unre-
> lated.
> Avoid the subject of contention.
> Do nothing and carry on as usual.
> Ignore the apparent problem for a time until you feel ready to
> handle it.

3. *Developing capacity to deal with the problem:* which included:
> Leave margins of time between activities.
> Try to get as much rest as possible so you will be fresh and alert
> for work.
> Throw yourself into work and work longer and harder.
> Become more involved in non-work activities – hobbies, leisure,
> etc.

4. *Rationalising the problem,* which included:
> Simply remember that there are others in worse situations than
> yours.
> Get support from the fact that not all problems can be solved,
> even at national level.
> Accept that it's your job and do it.
> Reconsider just how involved you are in your work.

5. *Support through spiritual commitment,* which included:
> Share the problem with prayer group.
> Share in the support group of the Church.
> Continually renew commitment to Christ.
> Take a break – have a quiet time every day.

These coping processes do seem to be aimed more at reducing the
levels of emotional discomfort which may result from the stressors, than
attacking the source of the stress: they are palliative 'emotion-focused'
strategies. Dewe suggests that this is because, in the main, the stressors
in a cleric's job are largely outside his control (as is often the case with
occupations which may be susceptible to burnout). He suggests that
'there may be little, if anything, many ministers can do to deal directly
with certain stressors. Thus strategies which allow for the dissipation or
regulation of emotional discomfort should be viewed as a legitimate
part of coping and an important facet of our coping repertoire.'[17]
    Not all research studies, however, support the view that the job of
clergymen/women is stressful. If one considers objective indices of

strain such as coronary heart disease risk, for example, the opposite appears to be the case. Holme, Helgeland, Hjerman, Leren and Lund-Larsen[18] assessed symptom-free 40–49-year-old men living in Oslo for coronary risk factors: raised serum cholesterol, triglycerides, blood pressure, smoking and body weight. A multiplicative risk score was computed for each of the 43 occupations considered. Those in religious work had by far the lowest coronary risk score (a mean of 4.1 compared to an average of 10.2).

Objective evidence from occupational mortality statistics of England and Wales shows that clergy have a good life expectancy. For example the Standardised Mortality Ratio (SMR) of Clergy, Ministers of Religion, for men aged 20–64 years, is only 70 (100 is average, and figures lower than 100 demonstrate fewer deaths than expected). Table 2.1 shows the mortality risks in clergy for the major causes of death for two mortality statistics, the SMR and the Proportional Mortality Ratio (PMR).[19] The table shows that clergy have low mortality rates for most causes, which would support the view that their job is not particularly stressful. They do, however, show particular elevations for cancer of the colon, cancer of the brain, cancer of the lymph and haematopoietic tissue and chronic liver disease and cirrhosis.[20] Whether this may be due to some other aspect of the lifestyle of clergy is another matter.

Table 2.1 Mortality rates of clergy, ministers of religion (occupation unit number 014), males, aged 20–64, 1979–80 and 1982–83, for different causes of death. The * symbol indicates a significant deviation from 100.

Cause of death	SMR	PMR
ALL CAUSES	70	100
Infectious and parasitic diseases	42	60
Neoplasms (all)	67*	96
Digestive organs and peritoneum	75*	108
Stomach	48	69
Colon	128	184*
Trachea, bronchus and lung	27*	38*
Brain	124	180*
Lymph and haematopoietic tissue	138	200*
Endocrine, nutritional diseases etc.	62	89
Diseases of circulatory system	78*	112*
Hypertensive diseases	53	76
Ischaemic heart disease	83	119*
Acute myocardial infarction	87*	125*
Cerebrovascular disease	71*	103
Diseases of respiratory system	36*	51*
Diseases of digestive system	68	98
Chronic liver disease and cirrhosis	131	191*
Diseases of genitourinary system	51	74
External causes, injury and poisoning	53*	78
Motor vehicle accidents	57	83
Suicide and self-inflicted	47	69

Abstracted from OPCS Occupational Mortality Microfiche tables, Series DS, no. 6, HMSO, 1986.

Other psychologically oriented studies suggest that clergy are exposed to *less* stress than the average person at work. Rayburn, Richmond and Rogers,[21] for example, studied the stressors and strains of 250 religious leaders (50 Roman Catholic priests, 50 brothers, 50 nuns, 50 ministers and 50 seminarians) and 549 individuals who formed a normative comparison group. They were all given a Religion and Stress Questionnaire and an occupational stressors and strains questionnaire. In addition, 10 per cent of the sample were given in-depth interviews. The Religion and Stress Questionnaire revolved around issues relating to the extra difficulties women were shown to experience in their role as clergy (although clergywomen thought they handled work-related stress better than clergymen mainly because they are more open about their feelings). The other questionnaires generally showed that, compared to the normative group, the religious professionals experienced significantly less stress. For example, they showed much less role insufficiency (the degree of misfit between training/skills and the work they have to do), fewer problems at role boundaries (conflict between role demands of job and loyalties at work), less stress from the physical work environment (extreme physical conditions or toxic exposure). There was also a tendency (not statistically significant) for the religious professionals to show less role overload (demands exceeding resources), role ambiguity (lack of job clarity) and responsibility (for the welfare of others). The results also revealed that the clergy showed less vocational strain, psychological strain, physical strain and interpersonal strain than the general population. Questions relating to personal resources did confirm Lauer's[22] finding that clergy have less leisure or recreational time than others, and the results also suggested that they have fewer rational/cognitive coping resources, were less likely to set and follow priorities, more distractible, less likely to have a systematic problem-solving approach, and less likely to put the job out of their minds when they go home. Overall, however, the religious professionals reported more personal resources to counteract the effects of occupational stress compared to the normative sample.

What these studies demonstrate in relation to the stressors and strains of Church of England clergy is unclear at best. For example, parochial clergy may have more varied demands placed upon them than nuns and brothers, and there are certainly differences between the stress levels of the different types of cleric. In the Rayburn, Richmond and Rogers study[23] the ministers (the group most similar to Church of England parochial clergy) showed the greatest overall stress, the most work overload, the highest role insufficiency, role ambiguity, responsibility and vocational strain. They were also the second highest of the religious groups on psychological, personal, physical and overall personal strain.

It does seem likely that parochial clergy are susceptible to burnout, but no strong evidence shows that this is the case in the Church of England. Moreover, given the conflicting evidence that has been presented above, and the doubts that such evidence could be of great relevance to the position of Church of England clergy, it seemed necessary to conduct a specifically designed research project in England and Wales. This study is reported below. It should be noted that it is a self-report, or questionnaire study, and the measures and theoretical backcloth used were based on previous stress research. This allows for comparative analyses with other working groups, as well as providing for the use of more validated measures. The project provides a picture of the stressors which parochial clergy perceive as being most important for them, it gives an estimate of the number of clergy who could really be said to be suffering from strain, and provides a first-stage analysis of the possible causes of the strain levels. It is also a questionnaire study based on a random sample of all parochial clergy in the Church of England, which strengthens the case for its findings being representative of the overall position. To my knowledge no other study of this nature has been done.

The study of parochial clergy in the Church of England

In late 1988, 372 questionnaires were sent to full-time parochial clergy in the Church of England, to every 51st suitable name from *Crockford's*, beginning at a random point. The questionnaire was relatively lengthy – consisting of more than 125 questions in 14 different sections:

1. *Background personal details*, which included age, marital status, stipendiary type, children, wife's employment if any, parish working expenses, churchmanship, and whether theological outlook was influenced by the Charismatic Renewal Movement.

2. *Quantitative workload*, which consisted of seven questions to assess *objective* indices of the amount of work each of the clergy was required to do, questions asked about the number of places of worship the person was responsible for, how many services they took each Sunday on average, the number of Parochial Church Councils, the extent, if any, of secretarial support, the number of occasional offices (funerals,

marriages, etc.) per month, the number of meetings in the parsonage house per week. This section also included a question on how often, if at all, the clergy felt rushed off their feet.

3. *Role expectations and ambiguities*, which consisted of five questions asking whether the parish paid its full quota, and about the pressure put on clergy by the diocesan authorities to ensure the full quota is paid, the extent to which they felt important diocesan policy decisions were made without reference to them, the extent to which the clergy felt uncertain about the exact authority over them held by the diocesan bishop, archdeacon, rural dean and diocesan administrators, and the perceived ambiguity between work and social roles.

4. *Role conflict.* Although the major role of the parochial minister is as preacher and teacher of the Christian faith, and administrator of the sacraments (as defined at ordination), the practical requirements of the job, and the roles required by parish priest, are much broader and often not understood by the general public. This section consisted of six questions concerning whether clergy felt the peripheral aspects of the job take over from the central role, the extent to which they felt other people's perception of their job was different from their own, how often, if at all, they felt that society does not value their job, and the conflict they experience between the roles of priest/parent, priest/husband, and priest/friend.

5. *Job demands* consisted of 22 statements which were possible sources of demands in the job. Clergy had to rate each one on a 1–5 scale to indicate the extent to which that aspect applied to them (if the factor was not a relevant aspect of their job they were required to indicate this with a '0' response). This section provided, therefore, a profile of the parochial minister's job in terms of perceived relevant demandingness. The 22 statements attempted to cover the whole gamut of potential demands followed in earlier studies.[24]

6. *Job supports–constraints.* The demands–supports model of stress proposes that the degree of strain experienced by the job incumbent is affected by the presence of support factors (or absence of constraints) which are relevant to coping with the demands placed upon them. This section consisted of 23 statements concerning possible supports–constraints which clergy had to consider in terms of the degree to which it made their job easier or more difficult, on a 1–5 scale, with a '0' category if it was not relevant.[25]

7. *Disillusionment with parochial ministry* was assessed by nine questions which asked how frequently clergy felt they were dissatisfied with attendance in church on Sundays, whether they felt mid-week activities were too poorly attended, whether they felt their sermons were listened to carefully, how much they would encourage people to think of ordained ministry as their Christian vocation, the extent to which they felt others were prepared to praise or condemn the things they did, how much they felt society in general, and their church-going parishioners in particular, considered their job irrelevant, and how often, if at all, they felt they could not cope with the thought of being in the parochial ministry all their working life. One of the questions asked them whether they felt the Church thinks more of its administrators and sector ministers than of the parochial ministry.

8. *Self-esteem* was measured by a single item which asked the extent to which the clergy felt any lack of response to their efforts in work was attributable to their own failings.

9. *Job satisfaction* was measured by a single multiple-choice item which asked clergy about how much they had considered and desired alternative occupations. This format was taken from the study of teacher stress by Fletcher and Payne.

10. *Relationships with significant others* looked at how satisfied the clergy were with the working relationships with (i) the church wardens, (ii) the parochial Church Councils, (iii) the bishop, and (iv) other clergy. For each category the clergy were asked to rate their relationship on a 1–6 scale where 6 = completely dissatisfied and 1 = completely satisfied.

11. *Felt pressure of work* consisted of a single multiple-choice item from Fletcher and Payne. Since some pressure in a job may be considered a good thing, this section attempted to distinguish between positive pressure, pressure which was deemed stressful, and too little pressure.

12. *Adequacy of pay.* The stipends of clergy are not very generous and it was felt important to determine the degree to which perceived adequacy of pay might affect stress. A single multiple-choice item asked clergy how adequate they found their pay for providing the things they wanted, differentiating such aspects as saving, meeting bills, having holidays, getting into debt, and buying basics.

13. *Physical health* was assessed by five statements. Clergy were asked to say how often each of the statements applied to them on a 4-point scale

(1 = never, 4 = very frequently). Two items referred to actual physical exercise taken, two to perceived fitness, and one to frequency of suffering colds, flu or other physical illness.

14. *Psychological health and well-being* consisted of 27 items to measure general or free-floating anxiety, depression, and somatic anxiety. Twenty-four of the items were taken from Crown and Crisp's *Experiential Index* (CCEI),[26] although the response scale was modified to be consistent with section 13. Free-floating anxiety is general anxiety without a specific focus or object for the anxiety; depression includes such feelings as sadness, feeling like crying, and feeling that life is too much effort; somaticism refers to over-awareness or concern about bodily functions such as sweating, sleep disturbances and palpitations.

The results

Of the 372 questionnaires, 230 were returned (an excellent response rate of 62 per cent), which provided 216 usable cases. Because no information is available about the non-respondents (the questionnaires were anonymous and no follow-up was, therefore, possible) it will be assumed that the returned sample is representative of the position of parochial clergy in general. In this section the descriptive statistics and tabulations will be presented first, with the detailed analysis of the interrelationships between variables at the end of the chapter.

General information

The great majority of the respondents were incumbents (78 per cent), with 4 per cent being priests-in-charge, 8 per cent team vicars, 4 per cent curates in charge of a daughter church, and 6 per cent curates. The clergy were not very young, with only 19 per cent being under 40 years old, 27 per cent between 40 and 49, 34 per cent 50–59, and 20 per cent over 60 years old. This would suggest a severe shortage of ministers in the relatively near future unless the Church of England can attract a considerable number of younger people to the ordained ministry.

Most of the clergy were married (87 per cent) with 54 per cent having children financially dependent upon them (62 per cent of those who were married). Over one-third (36 per cent) said their wives were in paid employment and 25 per cent said they had private income apart from the household salaries.

These factors may partly explain the relatively high levels of felt adequacy of pay despite the low levels of financial remuneration from Church of England stipends: 16 per cent said their pay was 'completely adequate', 44 per cent found it 'very adequate (meets all my bills, buy things I want, etc.)', 25 per cent 'adequate'. However, a sizeable minority (14 per cent) admitted they found their pay 'inadequate', to the extent that they struggled to pay bills and frequently went into debt. It is worth pointing out that in two other studies using the same measure, only 4 per cent of teachers and 4 per cent of London taxi drivers reported their pay inadequate.[27] Not surprisingly, felt inadequacy of pay was significantly higher for married than single men (a mean of 2.4 versus 2.1). Pay inadequacy was greatest for clergy who had dependent children, whether or not their wives were in paid employment (mean score of 2.6). Those without dependent children obviously felt considerably better off (mean of 1.0 if wife working, and 0.8 if wife not working). Interestingly, 80 per cent of the clergy said their parishes paid their working expenses in full, suggesting the majority of clergy are not having to meet such expenses from their own income.

The clergy were asked about their churchmanship. Thirty-four per cent said it was Catholic, 18 per cent Liberal, and 29 per cent Evangelical. They were also questioned about the extent to which their theological outlook was influenced by the Charismatic Renewal Movement. Sixty-eight per cent admitted to being influenced to some degree (9 per cent 'a great deal', 18 per cent 'quite a lot', 41 per cent 'to some extent') and the highest proportion of these were of Evangelical churchmanship (40 per cent).

Quantitative overload

Table 2.2 shows the responses to the questions concerned with objective measures of workload.

Table 2.2 Quantitative workload

How many places of worship are you responsible for?
  1 = 47%; 2 = 29%; 3 = 11%; More than 3 = 13%.
How many services do you take on an average Sunday?
  1 = 2%;   2 = 20%; 3 = 57%; More than 3 = 21%.
How many individual Parish Church Councils do you have?
  1 = 64%; 2 = 18%; 3 = 11%; More than 3 = 7%.
What secretarial help do you have?
  Full-time = 1%; regular part-time = 21%; occasional = 23%;
  None at all = 55%.
How many occasional offices do you take in a month?
  1–5 = 40%; 6–10 = 33%; 11–15 = 14%; More than 15 = 11%.
How many meetings do you have in the parsonage house in an average week?
  1 = 52%; 2 = 24%; 3 = 11%; More than 3 = 9%.
How often do you feel rushed off your feet?
  Hardly ever = 12%; sometimes = 42%; frequently = 41%;
  very frequently = 4%.

(Numbers may not add up to 100% due to missing answers.)

Each of the questions was scored on a 1–4 scale in which 4 indicated the highest workload. Thus, the maximum possible score for all questions added together was 28 and the minimum 7. No respondent scored the maximum, although 8 per cent did score 21 or more (that is, an average of 3 for each question). The overall mean score was 15.9.

Role ambiguities

Role ambiguity refers to the person not having a clear enough idea about their role or the job they are doing. It can be due to such factors as uncertain lines of authority, lack of an adequate job description, lack of feedback or the 'fuzzy' boundaries of the job. Table 2.3 presents the responses of the clergy to some of these questions.

Table 2.3 Ambiguities in parochial ministry

Do you find it difficult to distinguish between work and socialising?
Not at all = 14%;   not very frequently = 39%;   frequently = 38%;
very frequently = 7%.

Do you feel that important diocesan decisions are made without reference to the parochial clergy?
Never = 9%;   sometimes = 51%;   most of the time = 33%;
always = 5%.

What pressure, if any, is put upon you by the diocesan authorities to make sure the quota is paid?
None at all = 24%;   some = 48%;   quite a lot = 18%;   a lot = 7%.

Do you ever feel it would be helpful to know the exact authority, if any, the diocesan bishop, the archdeacon, the rural dean and the diocesan administrators have over you?
Never = 34%;   not very frequently = 51%;   frequently = 11%;
very frequently = 3%.

Role conflicts

People can have different expectations concerning their role compared to what others expect of them. Classically, role conflict occurs where an individual is asked to do things which are in conflict with some other job function, or where the role they are asked to perform is at odds with what they believe, or with some other role they should fulfil. Six items measured different types of potential conflict on a 3-point scale (3 = frequent conflict) and the frequency of each response obtained is shown in Table 2.4.

Table 2.4 Conflicting roles in parochial ministry

Do you feel that peripheral areas of your job take over from your primary role?
  Never = 6%; sometimes = 53%; frequently = 41%.

Do you feel that other people's perceptions of what your job is are different from your own?
  Never = 0%; sometimes = 39%; frequently = 60%.

Do you feel that society at large does not consider your job important?
  Never = 8%; sometimes = 57%; frequently = 34%.

Do the following roles ever conflict in your own mind?
Priest/Parent:
  Never = 26%; sometimes = 45%; frequently = 14%.
Priest/Husband:
  Never = 20%; sometimes = 47%; frequently = 21%.
Priest/Friend:
  Never = 30%; sometimes = 56%; frequently = 12%.

A composite score for role conflict was obtained by summing the scores on each of the six questions, making a maximum possible score of 18. The mean score obtained for all clergy was 12.3. Three individuals scored the maximum, and 20 per cent scored in excess of 15, suggesting quite high levels of felt role conflict.

Job satisfaction

Job satisfaction was assessed in terms of the clergy's attitudes to full-time ministry viewed as the job, not as their God-given vocation. The clergy were clearly very satisfied with their jobs overall, as is shown by the responses from this item in Table 2.5.

Table 2.5 Job satisfaction levels of the clergy

(Clergy were asked to tick one of the phrases which best represented their feelings about their job)

I feel it is a worthwhile job and would not dream of doing anything else.	53%
I feel it is a worthwhile job, but I wouldn't mind doing something else for a living.	20%
I feel it is a worthwhile job, but I can think of lots of other jobs I would like to do.	8%
I feel it is a worthwhile job, but the Church should look seriously at alternatives to full-time ministry.	14%
I feel it is a worthwhile job, but it's not for me and I would get out if I could.	1%
I think it is a worthwhile job, but I dislike it very much and would dearly love to do something else.	2%

If this item is scored on a 1–6 scale (where 6 = very dissatisfied) the mean score for the clergy is 1.95 and constitutes very high satisfaction levels. The fact that 53 per cent 'would not dream of doing anything else' could be due to very high vocational commitment, rather than satisfaction *per se*, and is something the Church of England should not, as an employer, be too ready to interpret positively. This is especially so when considering the scores obtained for self-esteem and job disillusionment.

Job disillusionment

Aspects of job disillusionment considered important to measure are shown in Table 2.6, together with the percentages of clergy who used each of the three response categories for each question.

Table 2.6 Aspects of disillusionment of parochial clergy

Feeling that mid-week activities, such as communions, house groups and prayer groups are poorly attended:
    Never = 3%;   sometimes = 53%; frequently = 43%.

Feeling that people do not listen very carefully to sermons:
    Never = 13%;   sometimes = 76%; frequently = 10%.

Feeling that people are slow to praise the good things you do and quick to condemn the bad:
    Never = 13%;   sometimes = 67%; frequently = 18%.

Feeling that you cannot cope with the thought of being in parochial ministry all your working life:
    Never = 40%;   sometimes = 49%; frequently = 10%.

To what extent would you encourage people to think of full-time ordained ministry as their Christian vocation?
    A lot = 25%;   quite a lot = 58%; not at all = 14%.

The mean score obtained by summing the responses to each of the five questions on the 1–3 scale was 9.9 out of a maximum of 15, with 5 per cent scoring either the maximum or one less, and 7 per cent 7 or less.

Self-esteem

How people feel about themselves may affect their health and well-being in addition to how they perceive their job, other situations and people. Five questions, again using a 3-point response scale, attempted to assess how the clergy perceived themselves, and how they felt other agencies (for example parishioners, the Church) evaluated them. The pattern of responses is shown in Table 2.7.

Table 2.7 The self-esteem of parochial clergy

Do you feel that an apparent lack of response in others is your own fault?
Never = 5%; sometimes = 81%; frequently = 26%.

Do you ever feel that society at large considers your job irrelevant?
Never = 11%; sometimes = 61%; frequently = 28%.

Do you ever feel that your church-going parishioners think your job is irrelevant?
Never = 59%; sometimes = 37%; frequently = 4%.

Do you ever feel dissatisfied with the number of people you get in church on a Sunday?
Never = 6%; sometimes = 68%; frequently = 26%.

Do you ever feel that the Church thinks more of its administrators and sector ministers than it does of parochial ministry?
Never = 27%; sometimes = 42%; frequently = 28%.

As can be seen from the table, something of the order of one-quarter or less of the clergy seemed to be relatively low in self-esteem, although overall this figure suggests a relatively healthy state of affairs (one might even suggest some complacency). Scoring on a 3-point scale in which a high figure is consistent with low self-esteem, the mean score for the section when the scores are summed across questions was 9.8, with no clergy showing a maximum score, 8 per cent scoring 13 or 14 (low self-esteem), and 23 per cent 8 or less (high self-esteem).

Relationships with significant others

The role other individuals play in stress can be very marked. For example, every organisation has its 'stress carriers' who, rather like the carriers of some diseases, infect others with stress although they do not show the symptoms themselves. Interpersonal factors also play a significant role in social support which may also buffer the effects of work stressors. The questionnaire investigated clergy satisfaction with relationships in four areas of 'significant others': bishops, wardens, the Parochial Church Council members, and 'other clergy'. The clergy rated each on a 6-point scale where 1 indicated 'completely satisfied' and 6 indicated 'completely dissatisfied'. Table 2.8 presents the frequency counts for each response category on each question.

Table 2.8 Satisfaction with relationships with significant others

		Bishop	PCC	Other clergy	Church wardens
Completely satisfied =	1	18%	16%	8%	53%
Very satisfied =	2	25%	26%	24%	20%
Pretty satisfied =	3	22%	27%	26%	8%
Satisfied =	4	18%	18%	25%	14%
Dissatisfied =	5	10%	12%	13%	1%
Completely dissatisfied =	6	7%	1%	4%	2%

The mean scores for each of the categories were: satisfaction with bishops, 3; with PCCs, 2.8; with other clergy, 3.2; and church wardens, 2.3. On the whole clergy are well satisfied with how they get on with their church wardens, and they show quite high levels of satisfaction with the other categories too, although a sizeable minority (7 per cent) are completely dissatisfied with their relationship with the bishop. One might, perhaps, have expected other clergy to have been viewed in more positive terms, although geographic factors might be playing a role here.

Felt pressure of work

Pressure or demand may be perceived as being stressful. On the other hand, some people prefer a very active job with a fair degree of pressure. Selye,[28] for example, makes the distinction between what he calls 'distress', or negative pressure, and 'eustress' or positive pressure. Research has also indicated that having too little pressure or stimulation in the job can produce marked strain in terms of increased excretion of the stress hormones adrenalin and noradrenalin,[29] and Selye has also distinguished another strain axis by differentiating 'hyperstress' (too much) from 'hypostress' (too little). In determining how much pressure the clergy felt themselves to be under, therefore, it was important to establish their reaction to it as well. The clergy were asked how they felt about the pressure in parochial ministry with a single multiple-choice question. The alternatives, and the pattern of responses, are shown in Table 2.9. For comparative purposes the table also shows the figures from a study of stress in teachers which revealed quite high levels of psychopathological disorders.

Table 2.9 How clergy felt about the pressure of parochial ministry compared to a sample of teachers.[30]

	Clergy	Teachers
There is little pressure and I frequently feel fed up or bored	2%	4%
Now and again I wish I was a bit more pressured	4%	
There is a little pressure which is part and parcel of the job and it makes the job more enjoyable	17%	25%
There is a lot of pressure but I actually enjoy it	14%	23%
There is a lot of pressure but I find I can cope	58%	44%
The pressure is so great it is a constant source of stress to me	5%	4%

The table reveals that although 77 per cent of the clergy felt the job was very pressured (a figure which would probably surprise the lay public), only 5 per cent found the pressure a constant source of stress (with a further 2 per cent suffering apparent hypostress). The felt pressure was higher than that obtained in the teacher sample (using a 1–6 scale, with 6 as maximum pressure) with a mean score of 4.4 compared to 4.1.

The psychological health of parochial clergy

We have seen that a significant number of clergy feel negative about a number of aspects of their job. What, however, is the state of their psychological health in terms of depression, somatic anxiety and free-floating anxiety? In a real sense this is the true barometer of whether or not the clergy are suffering from the effects of work stress. Overall the figures were very encouraging. In terms of depression only 5 per cent of the clergy were scoring on the CCEI scale at what could be considered 'case' levels, suggesting a definite and disabling dysfunction. A further 11 per cent were classified as showing minor dysfunction: they could be said to have depressive tendencies if the circumstances were to become more stressful. These percentages are below estimates one would expect to see in an ordinary working population.[31] The figures for free-floating anxiety were even better, only 2 per cent scoring at case level and a further 7 per cent at the lower criterion. Less than 0.5 per cent showed elevated scores on the somaticism scale, with less than 3 per cent at the borderline level.

The perception of job demands amongst parochial clergy

The 22 demand items were rated according to a 5-point scale, where 5 represented greatest demand. Clergy could also use a '0' score if the item was not relevant in their circumstances. The ranked ordered demands, with mean demand scores, the percentage of clergy who gave each demand a 5-rating, and the percentage for whom it was rated 0 or 'not relevant' are shown in Table 2.10.

Table 2.10 The ratings of each job demand by parochial clergy

Demand	Mean score	% 5 rating	% 4	% 'not relevant'
Having to satisfy expectations of others	3.5	15	42	2
Being on call 24 hours per day	3.3	11	41	1
Parish success or failure my responsibility alone	3.2	14	34	2
Expectation that I will attend to others' needs immediately	3.2	11	37	1
Frequently being in positions of potential conflict	3.1	11	31	1
Always having to please other people	3.1	10	32	1
Insufficient financial resources to do job	3.0	10	31	5
Lack of tangible results	2.9	7	32	3
Feeling others are always passing judgement on me	2.8	5	24	2
Having my home constantly used by others	2.8	4	20	4
Necessary involvement of my family in my work	2.7	7	24	7
Role not readily recognised by society	2.7	7	19	3
Having to be nice to people	2.7	6	23	3
The feeling that I must be liked for people to attend church	2.7	4	23	4
Not having a set routine	2.6	6	22	2
Expectation that I have no right to reply to criticism	2.6	5	14	2
Rarely being thanked for things I do	2.5	4	14	4
Feeling the Church hierarchy does not value parochial ministry	2.4	9	13	2
Being expected to have leading secular role	2.4	3	11	5
Feeling others do not care for me	2.4	3	12	3
Having to stand and preach every Sunday	2.3	2	22	2
Being isolated from other clergy	2.1	3	8	3

Table 2.10 does not, of course, show the demands which may result from the factors such as role ambiguity, role overload or conflict, which have already been presented above. It does suggest that the expectations of others are a major demand, primarily focusing around having to put on a 'public face' and acting 'in role' while at the same time not being valued for perceived worth. Inadequate financial resources also cause considerable demand for about one in ten clergy. Moreover, although generally rated as not demanding by many clergy (hence its low mean score) 9 per cent of them felt that the Church hierarchy (bishops, administrators and church commissioners) did not value parochial ministry to a marked degree sufficient to make the job demanding. The small number of 'not relevant' responses also shows that the items clergy were asked to rate were generally appropriate to them. The average demand scores were not particularly high: only seven items resulted in a mean above 3 (the mid-point). It should also be noted that only 2 per cent of the clergy obtained an average score across all items of more than 4 (i.e. a total in excess of 87), although some specific items (those seven at the top of Table 2.10) were consistently rated highly demanding by 10 per cent or more of clergy.

Job supports and constraints

The stressors of parochial ministry are unlikely to be the only aspects which determine the health and well-being of the clergy. As discussed in Chapter 1, the supports and constraints of parochial work will also play a role. For example, the social support received from parishioners and family, the large degree of autonomy to order the working week, and the pleasure from doing a worthwhile job (albeit possibly in difficult and constraining circumstances), are all potential buffers to reduce the negative effects of the stressors. The perceived importance to clergy of the 23 job supports–constraints measured in the survey are presented in Table 2.11. The clergy were asked to rate whether, and to what degree, their job was made harder (a constraint) or easier (a support) by each item. The table gives the mean score on the 5-point scale for each item as well as the number of clergy who rated it a constraint (i.e. a score of 1 or 2), a marked support (i.e. a score of 5), or did not see it as having any effect on their job (i.e. a score of 0).

As can be seen from Table 2.11, almost all the sampled items were considered to act as supports for the majority of clergy (it should be remembered that the question asks them to consider each item in terms of how it impinges on their *job*). Supports from wife and family were considered very important, with very few clergy considering them constraining. Some 45 per cent of clergy received great support from knowing they were doing a worthwhile job, and over one-quarter benefited markedly from the freedom and autonomy of parochial life. Being able to pray in small groups was a clear benefit for over one-third of clergy, although one in ten also perceived it of no benefit (or cost) to their job. The church officers of the clergy were well regarded by nearly one-quarter of clergy, although the PCC officers were considered constraining by 8 per cent. The level of remuneration was considered a constraint by 31 per cent, which was by far the highest percentage for a job constraint. Living in the parsonage house/using it as an office was supportive for some 15 per cent of clergy, although slightly more (18 per cent) found it definitely constraining in their work: clearly one needs to consider both costs and benefits in such circumstances. In general, the bishop/archdeacon/rural dean was perceived to be largely irrelevant to work matters by about one-third of clergy although a significant minority of 14 per cent found them supportive. The sector ministries had little impact on everyday work.

Table 2.11 The supports–constraints in parochial ministry

Support–constraint item	mean score	% 5-rating	% 1/2 rating	% no effect
Encouragement and help from wife	4.3	50	0	2
Feeling I am doing a worthwhile job	4.1	45	3	4
Being able to pray with a small group	3.8	34	1	10
Freedom I have in ordering my working day	3.8	26	3	3
Encouragement and help from my Church officers	3.8	23	2	3
Encouragement and help from family	3.7	32	1	12
Having job security	3.5	32	1	17
Encouragement and help from PCC	3.5	14	8	3
Encouragement and help from parishioners	3.5	13	3	3
Training received in first curacy	3.4	21	4	13
Living in a parsonage house	3.2	15	18	7
Having my office in the home	3.2	15	18	7
Training given at theological college	3.2	14	4	18
Intellectual challenge the work provides	3.2	11	8	11
Encouragement and help from full-time colleagues	3.1	18	2	19
Encouragement and help from diocesan administrators	3.0	10	9	18
Encouragement and support from bishop	2.8	14	5	27
Encouragement and support from archdeacon	2.6	13	6	30

Support–constraint item	mean score	% 5-rating	% 1/2 rating	% no effect
Encouragement and support from rural dean	2.5	14	5	32
The level of remuneration	2.5	8	31	16
Expectations of ministry fostered during training	2.5	7	8	25
Encouragement and help from 'sector ministries'	1.7	2	4	46
Amount of control over pay, pensions and conditions	1.7	2	18	41

Physical health

Five questions addressed aspects of physical well-being and bodily condition and each required a response on a 1–4 scale where 1 corresponded to 'never' and 4 to 'very frequently'. In response to 'suffering from colds, flu or other physical illness' 6 per cent gave a 4 answer. Seventeen per cent often felt dissatisfied with their body shape/size (although 30 per cent never did), and 18 per cent often felt unsupple and unfit. Some 73 per cent said they exercised at least now and again (38 per cent very frequently), and 35 per cent said they very frequently walked somewhere instead of using public transport. Overall, these figures suggest a relatively healthy perception of general health.

What aspects of work affect the well-being of parochial clergy?

We have seen how the average parochial clergyman perceives their work, what factors they think may affect their performance, and how they view themselves and their profession. The major question to be answered in stress research, however, is whether any of these factors affect health and well-being. This section addresses this question. There are a number of ways one can begin to tackle the issue. First, are the work factors associated with psychopathology in terms of depression, anxiety and somaticism which were measured in the questionnaire? Second, are other strains, such as job dissatisfaction, job disillusionment, self-esteem, and felt pressure of work (which may be precursors of psychopathology) associated with the aspects of work which were measured? Third, what is the relationship between the work stressors, affective and psychoneurotic scores, and the negative perceptions of the job (for example, job dissatisfaction, disillusionment)? These will be considered in turn.

The effects of work on psychopathology

The first step here is to consider whether there are any work factors which are associated with the depression, free-floating anxiety, and somatic anxiety scores. Table 2.12 presents a picture of which work factors were associated or statistically correlated[32] with all three of the measures of psychopathology to a level of confidence greater than 95 per cent that the associations were not due to chance. The factors shown in Table 2.12 are those which may play a role in causally determining psychological ill-health, although they are not specific in their effect (because they are associated with each kind of psychological dysfunction, not any one selectively).

Table 2.12 Possible causes of psychological ill-health among parochial clergy: factors which are significantly correlated with free-floating anxiety, depression and somaticism

Work factor	Correlation Size		
	Anxiety	Depression	Somaticism
ROLE AMBIGUITY TOTAL SCORE	0.16	0.20	0.19
Wanting to know the exact authority the diocesan bishop/archdeacon/ rural dean have	0.24	0.22	0.20
ROLE CONFLICT TOTAL SCORE	0.27	0.18	0.14
Role conflict between priest/husband	0.30	0.23	0.16
WORK DEMANDS TOTAL SCORE	0.51	0.45	0.36
Being on call 24 hours a day	0.20	0.14	0.19
Having to satisfy expectations of others	0.36	0.31	0.21
Not having a role recognised by society	0.28	0.26	0.16
Success/failure my responsibility alone	0.38	0.35	0.25
Always having to please other people	0.35	0.34	0.21
Being in positions of potential conflict often	0.38	0.34	0.38
Tension from having to involve family in work	0.24	0.20	0.14
Expectation to respond immediately to others	0.29	0.23	0.16
Need to be liked to get people in church	0.21	0.27	0.17
Being isolated from other clergy	0.18	0.17	0.21
Having to stand up and preach every Sunday	0.19	0.27	0.21

Work factor	Anxiety	Correlation Size Depression	Somaticism
People always passing judgement on me	0.37	0.27	0.29
Taking leading role in secular society	0.27	0.16	0.17
Having to be nice to people	0.38	0.36	0.17
Feeling others do not care for me	0.36	0.30	0.20
Rarely being thanked for what I do	0.28	0.24	0.20
Lack of tangible results	0.35	0.46	0.20
Feeling I cannot respond to criticism	0.37	0.47	0.36
WORK SUPPORT—CONSTRAINTS			
Encouragement and help from parishioners	—0.14	—0.23	—0.20
JOB DISILLUSIONMENT TOTAL SCORE	0.23	0.37	0.17
Poor attendance at mid-week activities	0.16	0.27	0.17
People slow to praise good/quick condemn bad	0.19	0.29	0.26
SELF-ESTEEM (LACK) TOTAL SCORE	0.22	0.31	0.25
Feeling lack of response in others is due to me	0.14	0.21	0.17
FELT PRESSURE OF WORK	0.25	0.22	0.18
POOR GENERAL PHYSICAL HEALTH	0.34	0.42	0.29
Dissatisfaction with relationships with:			
Bishop	0.13	0.21	0.17
PCC	0.21	0.25	0.23
Other clergy	0.28	0.21	0.23

It will be noted that all the correlations are in the predicted direction. Positive correlations show that an increase in the score on one variable is associated with an increase in the other variable (for example, a higher demand score is associated with a higher psychoneurotic or affective state score). Negative correlations indicate the opposite (for example, the higher the support score the lower the psychological ill-health).

Some of the work factors seemed to be more specific in their manifestation in psychopathology. For example, those who were more likely to feel that other people's perception of the job was different from their own were more likely to have higher depression scores,[33] but not higher anxiety or somaticism scores. Those clergy who feel society in general, and church-going parishioners in particular, do not consider the job important, or feel people do not listen carefully to their sermons, were also more likely to have higher depression scores.[34] Clergy who felt they received less support from their wives, or from using the home as an office, or those who did not feel they were performing a worthwhile job function, were also more likely to have elevated depression scores.[35] Higher, free-floating anxiety scores were associated with greater felt demand from having the home constantly used by others[36] and those who had less secretarial help.[37] Those with higher somatic anxiety reported less support from full-time colleagues,[38] from their Church officers,[39] from living in the parsonage house,[40] and less support from job security.[41] Job dissatisfaction was correlated with both anxiety and depression,[42] as was the demand of not having a set routine,[43] and the conflicting roles of priest/parent[44] and priest/friend.[45]

It is interesting to note that quantitative work overload showed little association with psychopathology. None of the psychoneurotic or affective scales were correlated with the total quantitative workload score, although those who took more services on a Sunday were more likely to score higher on somaticism[46] and both anxiety and somaticism scores were related to the number of weekly meetings in the parsonage house[47] and to how often clergy felt rushed off their feet.[48] It is also interesting to note that pay satisfaction was unrelated to psychopathology.

In order to demonstrate the relationship between the work stressors and psychopathology in a simple manner, Table 2.13 presents the scores on some of the variables measured when the clergy group is split according to how much strain they show. The high strain group are those who scored 20 or more on either of the three scales measuring anxiety, depression or somaticism (that is, an average score of 2.5 or more out of 4 for all eight items in that scale). The low strain group consists of those who scored less than 20 on all the scales. There were 58 clergy in the high strain group and 158 in the low strain group.

Factors related to job satisfaction and felt pressure of work

Factors such as job dissatisfaction, felt pressure of work and disillusionment with parochial ministry are themselves very important indicators of how clergy feel about important matters even if the minister is not suffering from a chronic psychopathological condition. They are also likely to play a role in affecting psychopathology and may mediate the relationship between work stressors and strain dysfunction. For example, if the minister is dissatisfied with his job for any length of time, or if he feels under considerable work pressure, this may well lead to strain conditions and also affect how the minister perceives all aspects of his job. This section shows which aspects of all those measured in the survey were associated with job dissatisfaction and felt pressure of work. Table 2.14 presents the significant correlations for job satisfaction and felt pressure of work. Remember that a higher score on job satisfaction indicates greater dissatisfaction, and a higher score on felt pressure indicates more stress.

Table 2.13 Differences between the HIGH and LOW STRAIN groups on selected variables (numbers shown are based on the scale scores)

	low strain	high strain
Number of meetings in parsonage house/week	1.6	2.0
JOB SATISFACTION	1.8	2.3
Dissatisfaction with relationships with bishop	2.9	3.4
Dissatisfaction with relationship with PCC	2.7	3.2
FELT PRESSURE OF WORK	4.3	4.6
JOB DISILLUSIONMENT TOTAL	9.6	10.8
SELF-ESTEEM	9.5	10.7
ROLE AMBIGUITY TOTAL	8.2	9.2
ROLE CONFLICT TOTAL	11.9	13.2
WORK SUPPORT TOTAL	72	67
JOB DEMANDS TOTAL	56	70
Having to satisfy the expectations of others	3.3	4.0
Success of parish dependent entirely on me	3.0	3.8
Always having to please other people	2.8	3.7
Frequently being in positions of potential conflict	2.9	3.7
Necessary involvement of family	2.6	3.2
Having to immediately respond to others' needs	3.1	3.6
Having to be liked for people to attend church	2.5	3.1
Preaching every Sunday	2.2	2.8
Others always passing judgement on me	2.6	3.4
The Church hierarchy not valuing parochial ministry	2.3	2.8
Having to play a leading role in secular society	2.3	2.7
Having to be nice to people	2.5	3.3
Lack of tangible results	2.7	3.5
Expectation of having no right of reply to criticism	2.2	3.3

Table 2.14 Work factors related to job satisfaction and felt pressure of work (ns = not statistically significant)

Work factor	Job satisfaction	Felt pressure of work
Number of occasional offices/month	ns	0.14
Number of meetings in parsonage house/week	—0.14	0.17
Feeling rushed off feet	ns	0.29
ROLE AMBIGUITY TOTAL SCORE	0.18	ns.
Feeling diocesan decisions made without reference to parochial clergy	0.20	ns.
Feeling it would be helpful to know exact authority of diocesan bishop/archdeacon/rural dean, etc.	ns	0.18
ROLE CONFLICT TOTAL SCORE	ns	0.21
Peripheral areas of job takeover	ns	0.20
Society does not consider job important	0.16	ns
Role conflict between priest/parent	ns	0.26
Role conflict between priest/husband	ns	0.26

Work factor	Job satisfaction	Felt pressure of work
JOB DEMANDS TOTAL SCORE	0.21	0.27
Being on call 24 hours/day	ns	0.22
Having to always satisfy expectations of others	ns	0.22
Success or failure depends on me	ns	0.14
Always having to please other people	0.14	0.15
Frequently being in positions of potential conflict	ns	0.25
Having to respond immediately to others' needs	0.14	0.19
Having to be liked for people to attend church	ns	0.21
Isolation from other clergy	ns	0.17
Having to preach every Sunday	0.17	ns
Feeling others always passing judgement on me	ns	0.24
Feeling Church hierarchy does not value parochial ministry	0.16	ns
Having to be nice to people	0.19	ns
Lack of tangible results	0.23	0.16
Expectation of having no right to reply to criticism	0.15	0.23
Having no set routine	0.16	0.23
JOB SUPPORTS TOTAL SCORE	—0.23	ns
Encouragement and help from Church officers	—0.16	ns
Encouragement and help from PCC	—0.19	ns
Encouragement and help from parishioners	—0.24	ns
Encouragement and help from wife	—0.18	ns
Training received at theological college	—0.18	ns
Living in the parsonage house	—0.19	ns
Being able to pray in small groups	—0.19	ns
Feeling I am doing a worthwhile task	—0.36	ns
SATISFACTION WITH RELATIONSHIPS WITH		
Bishop	0.21	ns
PCC	0.14	ns
Other clergy	0.23	ns
Church wardens	0.19	ns
JOB DISILLUSION TOTAL SCORE	0.32	ns
Extent to which encourage people to think of ordained ministry as their Christian vocation	0.35	—0.14
Feeling could not cope with parochial ministry all working life	0.48	ns

A number of aspects of Table 2.14 are worthy of comment. It will be noticed that the number of meetings each week in the parsonage house is related to both job satisfaction and felt pressure of work, but in opposite directions. One might have expected that those reporting fewer meetings would report less felt pressure, but also that this would be related to lower job satisfaction. However, the —0.14 correlation indicates that those reporting *fewer* meetings were *less* satisfied (this was the only correlation to be in the non–predicted direction). Perhaps the interpretation of this finding is that those with fewer meetings are less satisfied because they do not perceive themselves to be as much a part of the community and have integrated less well. The parsonage house is clearly the focus of both positive benefits to clergy (it is seen as a support) as well as the cause of negative effects (for example, those who perceived their home as constantly being used by others were more likely to have higher anxiety scores). It would seem important to minimise this potential conflict by separating the work and domestic roles more clearly, perhaps by having a definite 'consulting room/ office' with independent access.

Only one other measure of quantitative load was related to felt work pressure: the number of occasional offices held in a month, such that the more offices the higher the pressure. It should be recalled that this measure of load was also related to free-floating anxiety levels.

Role conflicts of various kinds seemed mainly to affect the felt pressure of work, although those who were less satisfied with their job were more likely to feel that society at large did not consider their job important. Many of the job demands were associated with felt pressure of work. However, job demands were not, in general, associated with job satisfaction (which, given the fact that they were related to psychopathology, reinforces the view that job satisfaction is a very misleading measure of job strain). A few job demands and some aspects of role ambiguity were correlated with job satisfaction, however. For example, those clergy who found it demanding to have to preach every Sunday, and those who felt the Church hierarchy does not value parochial ministry, were more likely to be less satisfied with their job although they did not also show more felt pressure.

Job supports showed no relationships with felt pressure of work, although they did appear to affect job satisfaction. The same was true for the effects of felt satisfaction with the relationships with the bishop, church wardens, other clergy and PCC. Given the correlations of these variables with depression, anxiety and somaticism, it appears that they may play an important role in mental well-being although the clergy may not realise the effects such factors may have in their well-being because they do not contribute to the degree of felt pressure.

The relationship between stressors, feelings about parochial ministry and strain

From the previous sections it is apparent that there are myriad significant relationships between the variables measured in the study. Interpreting the likely importance of each correlation must be done with great caution, for a number of reasons. For example, correlations are only measures of association and not of cause (although correlations may be present as a result of a causal relationship between two variables). Second, the study is a cross-sectional one (all variables measured at one time in every respondent). Such studies have their own strengths, but longitudinal studies are more effective for establishing causal relationships. Third, correlations can be difficult to interpret because apparently different variables are interrelated or confounded by other variables (I have elsewhere[49] made the distinction between primary and secondary stressors, where the latter are those which appear to be associated with the strain measure only because the person is stressed and has a lowered tolerance threshold). In the context of this study, for example, it may be the case that the effect of one job demand affects the perception of a whole array of other demands which make them appear important determinants of strain. It may also be the case that the demands determine the strain levels and these cause the person to become disillusioned with the job (rather than vice versa).

There are many such problems with all studies, however good, and the best tool to use when attributing cause and effect is undoubtedly a trained interpretive reason. There are, however, some sophisticated statistical tools which can aid sound interpretation. One set of such tools is based around multivariate procedures which allow many variables to be considered at once in order to determine the unique contribution any one variable makes, when the effects of the others are considered at the same time. A technique known as stepwise multiple regression was used here. This allows one to look at the relationships between a dependent variable (in this case the measures of depression and anxiety) and a set of possible predictor variables (for example, each job demand and support–constraint, role factors, self-esteem, job disillusionment, etc.). It allows the investigator to control for possible confounding between variables and provides some estimate of the separate and conjoint contribution of a number of the aspects of interest.

This tool was used to find the best predictors of depression from among the following variables: quantitative workload, role conflict, role ambiguity, job demands, job supports, job disillusionment and self-esteem. The analysis showed that job demands were the strongest independent associates of depression, although job disillusionment was also important. A similar analysis for anxiety again resulted in total job demands being revealed as the strongest predictor. In order to see which particular demands might be playing an important role in psycho-pathology separate analyses were made in which all the 22 individual demand items were considered simultaneously. For depression the results showed (in order of importance) the following demands:

EXPECTATION THAT I HAVE NO RIGHT TO REPLY TO CRITICISM
LACK OF TANGIBLE RESULTS
HAVING TO SATISFY EXPECTATIONS OF OTHERS
HAVING TO BE NICE TO PEOPLE

For anxiety the following demands were shown to be particularly important:

EXPECTATION THAT I HAVE NO RIGHT OF REPLY TO CRITICISM
FREQUENTLY BEING IN POSITIONS OF POTENTIAL CONFLICT
FEELING SUCCESS OF PARISH MY RESPONSIBILITY ALONE
HAVING TO BE NICE TO PEOPLE
LACK OF TANGIBLE RESULTS

Conclusions

The chapter has reviewed the previous evidence on stress among ministers of religion. Most of the research has been done in other countries and presented a somewhat contradictory picture. It appeared from that research that clergy might be particularly prone to burnout, although there was a clear need for an objective study of the position of parochial clergy in the Church of England. A study of over 200 parochial clergy in the Church of England was outlined. Most of the clergy were married incumbents, and the age profile showed that the majority were over 50 years old with more than half having children financially dependent upon them. Workloads for a substantial proportion of them were quite high. Over one-fifth took more than three services on an average Sunday, and 13 per cent were responsible for more than three places of worship. A quarter took eleven or more occasional offices per month, over half had no secretarial help at all for parish affairs, and there was considerable use of the parsonage household (which for some caused considerable difficulties). Over one-third of the clergy wives were in paid employment, although it was also clear that many wives were significant helpers in parish matters and provided the married clergy with considerable support in their work. Forty-five per cent of the clergy were at least 'frequently' rushed off their feet, with a similar number reporting significant role ambiguities. Conflicts of role in the job were also commonplace.

Overall the clergy were satisfied with their jobs, with only 3 per cent expressing a desire to get out of the ministry if they could. Over half would not dream of doing any other work. Despite this, many of the clergy were disillusioned with aspects of their job, such as poor attendance by parishioners, or people not listening to their sermons. Nearly 60 per cent had had the feeling that they could not cope with the thought of a life spent in parochial ministry, and self-esteem was not particularly high. Having to satisfy the expectations of others was a major demand, as was the feeling of being constantly on call. Seventeen per cent of the clergy were dissatisfied with their relationship with the bishop.

A significant proportion of the clergy were struggling to manage financially, although, on the other hand, more found their pay completely adequate for their needs. This discrepancy was probably the consequence of one-quarter who reported having some private income.

Many aspects of work were associated with experienced strain, and job demands and job disillusionment in particular seemed to play a role in depression and general anxiety. The job demands related to having to put on a public face; lack of tangible results and being in conflict situations were significant in this respect, although those with the highest levels of strain showed different perceptions on many different work factors compared to the clergy with lower levels of strain.

Overall, however, the objective measures of strain showed the clergy to be under less stress than one might expect. The percentages of clergy who scored at significantly elevated levels on the depression, free-floating anxiety, and somatic anxiety scales were very low indeed. Moreover, despite their obvious concerns about various aspects of their work, only 5 per cent found their job to be so pressured as to be a constant source of stress. It is difficult to determine whether the primary cause of strain in the strained minority has its focus in the person himself or his work situation. While such levels of strain are still higher than the ideal they do represent a relatively healthy state of affairs. It seems that parochial clergy are being stretched in a demanding job, but not one which is overtaxing the vast majority.

Notes

1. This research formed the basis of an MSc thesis at Hatfield Polytechnic completed by MacPherson (1989), and the findings were presented to the British Psychological Society (Fletcher and MacPherson, 1989).

2. Blackmon, 1984.

3. MacDonald, 1980.

4. Richmond, Rayburn and Rogers, 1985.

5. Maslach, 1978, 1982.

6. Daniel and Rogers, 1981; Doohan, 1982.

7. Hall and Gardner, 1979.

8. Swogger, 1981, p. 30.

9. Doohan, 1982, p. 353.

10. Daniel and Rogers, 1981.

11. Dunn, 1965, p. 133.

12. Lauer, 1973, p. 202.

13. *Ibid.*, p. 190.

14. *Ibid.*, pp. 194–5.

15. Warner and Carter, 1984.

16. Dewe, 1987.

17. *Ibid.*, p. 361.

18. Holme *et al.*, 1977.

19. From OPCS, 1986. This SMR is statistically lower than the average, with about 435 occupations (out of 556) having higher mortality rates. The figures in Table 2.1 are abstracted from the OPCS, 1986. The SMR is the ratio of clergy who died from a given cause to the number expected to have died from that cause given the age-specific mortality rates of the standard population. The PMR compares deaths due to a particular cause with that which would be expected from the proportions in the standard population. Thus a high PMR reflects not an excess mortality risk, but rather an excess proportion dying from a particular cause.

20. The raised PMRs could be due to clergy having lower than average rates for other causes of death, but for some causes additional information is available. Clergy do, it seems, have an elevated risk of dying from cancer of the colon: they have a very high Proportional Registration Ratio score of 275 (OPCS, 1986; Table 7.9). This measure is of new cancer registrations, and uses cancers, rather than all causes of death, as the base. Of course, these particular elevations are not likely to be due to work stress, even given the likely subtleties of stress which may be revealed in mortality statistics (Fletcher, 1988a, b).

21. Rayburn, Richmond and Rogers, 1986.

22. Lauer, 1973.

23. Rayburn, Richmond and Rogers, 1986.

24. Payne, 1979; Fletcher and Payne, 1982.

25. The statements attempted to cover a range of possible support–constraint factors relevant to parochial clergy and were the same type as used by Fletcher and Payne (1982) in their study of teacher stress, and Fletcher and Morris (1989) in a study of stress in taxi drivers.

26. Crown and Crisp, 1979.

27. Fletcher and Payne, 1982; Fletcher and Morris, 1989.

28. Selye, 1976.

29. Frankenhaeuser, 1975.

30. Fletcher and Payne, 1982.

31. Fletcher, 1988a.

32. The correlation statistic is a simple measure of association between two variables. The correlation

coefficient is a number between — 1 and +1, and the greater it deviates from zero, the stronger the association. A correlation coefficient of zero shows that variations in one variable are not associated with changes in the other; a statistically significant positive correlation shows that increments in one score are accompanied by increments in the other variable, while a negative correlation shows that increments in the score on one variable are accompanied by decrements in the other. To be statistically significant a sample of 216 requires a coefficient size of at least + or —0.135. Any coefficient of this size would be expected by chance only 5 times in 100 (in other words, there is a 95 per cent probability that it is a meaningful association). If the coefficient is larger, so the probability of it being a chance association becomes smaller. For example, a coefficient of + or —0.19 is significant to the $p < 0.005$ levels (that is, only 5 times in 1,000 would the result be obtained by chance), and a coefficient of greater than + or —0.26 is significant at the $p < 0.0001$ level.

33. The correlation was +0.17.
34. Correlations of +0.23, +0.21 and +0.17 respectively.
35. Correlations of —0.14, —0.14 and —0.18 respectively.
36. Correlation of +0.14.
37. Correlation of +0.15.
38. Correlation of —0.18.
39. Correlation of —0.18.
40. Correlation of —0.14.
41. Correlation of —0.13.
42. Correlations of +0.16 and +0.25 respectively.
43. Correlations of +0.24 and +0.20 respectively.
44. Correlations of +0.24 and +0.17 respectively.
45. Correlations of +0.27 and +0.26 respectively.
46. Correlation of +0.15.
47. Correlations of +0.13 and +0.14 respectively.
48. Correlations of +0.13 and +0.17 respectively.
49. See Fletcher and Payne, 1980b.

3

Stress and Homosexual Clergy: the Background

The pastoral care of clergy should be one of the primary functions of the Church of England. It is the employer of a large number of people: in 1987, for example, there were 10,624 full-time stipendiary clergy in the Church of England, of whom 8,199 were of incumbent status and 1,746 of assistant curate status.[1] If the sample of clergy who took part in the stress study in Chapter 2 is representative (they were a random sample) the Church would need to consider some of the findings carefully from a pastoral viewpoint. Given that 17 per cent of clergy are dissatisfied with their relationship with their bishop, this translates to more than 1,800 clergy; more than 530 clergy would also be under work-pressure of sufficient intensity as to be a constant source of stress to them.

Whether or not such statistics are a cause of concern for the Church is a matter for the Church. From the outside it does appear to be a caring employer which operates in an essentially Christian manner although it may not be sufficiently aware of the size of the problem. What is, perhaps, more problematic is the situation of homosexual clergy, who form a significant minority within the Church. These clergy may well be particularly prone to strain. This chapter assesses some of the reasons why this is so, and describes a pilot study to examine the stress levels of homosexual clergy.

The special difficulties for homosexual clergy

1. *Increased risk of psychopathology due to sexuality*. The Gloucester Report suggests that:

When we come to consider definite psychiatric disorders, a neurotic depressive reaction is common in homosexual people; this may be precipitated by conflict over being a homosexual person in a contemporary society, a broken sexual relationship, or some other stress not related to sexuality in any obvious way. It is not clear whether homosexual people are more prone to such reactions than the general population.[2]

There is some evidence that homosexual men are more vulnerable than heterosexuals to stress and, due to this, show elevated rates of substance abuse (alcohol, drugs, etc.,.[3] We will see later in this chapter and in Chapter 4 that homosexual clergy are more prone to strain reactions than the general population, or other clergy populations. Some writers propose that this is a result of problems of identity, or failure to find a satisfactory self-image due to 'society's failure to accept homosexuality as a legitimate variation of sexual drive... the gay person's principal problem becomes one of finding an acceptable identity within a hostile environment'.[4] It is doubtful that these higher strain levels are due primarily to inner conflicts (although see point 3 below), or broken relationships. It would seem more reasonable to attribute them to a constellation of interrelated factors, some internal, some to do with vocation, some to the difficulties of being a minority in society, some to do with external pressures (from the Church and others), and some to do with the normal stresses of everyday life which, because of the consequences of their sexuality, are more destructive. It has also been suggested that stressors in pregnancy may play a role in determining sexual orientation, perhaps because this stress affects the unborn child. For example, Ellis, Ames, Peckham and Burke[5] interviewed 285 women with offspring over 19 years of age. Retrospective accounts of stress and its severity in the period twelve months before pregnancy up to birth helped predict the sexual orientation of male offspring, with an apparent critical period during the second trimester. However, as well as the presence of negative forces, the homosexual clergy probably suffer more due to the relative absence of positive forces such as social support.

2. *Lack of adequate control and social support structures*. The importance of social support factors in strain has already been discussed in Chapter 1. Social support may provide an important buffer for the demands placed on an individual, or social factors might act to reduce the impact of demands by providing the individual with effective interpersonal coping processes. Such 'direct' or positive problem-focused coping is generally considered more effective than more

internalised emotion-focused palliatives.[6] While homosexual clergy, particularly in the cities, may have access to such things as gay clubs and other meeting places, it is unlikely that even their social networks for support will be as extensive as those of heterosexual priests. Of even greater potential importance, however, is that the vast majority of homosexual clergy do not have the benefits of being able to live with a partner. The study of parochial clergy outlined in Chapter 2 found that clergy saw wives and families as being a major source of support to them to cope with the effects of the job. Wives usually take on a significant and major work and social role in the parish, and this would not normally be possible for homosexual partners. Thus, the homosexual priest often has to distance himself somewhat from the community he is serving as well as from friends, other clergy, the bishop, etc. This is potentially very damaging psychologically, since the homosexual may be more caring (and requiring of reciprocation) than heterosexual clergy. Moreover, homosexual clergy, especially those in small parishes, are much less likely than their heterosexual counterparts to meet people with whom they can have frank and open discussions on matters of central importance to them: most have to hide behind a heterosexual veil and conduct conversations against a heterosexual backcloth.

The effective problem-focused coping strategies are more likely to be activated in situations where the individual perceives that there is something that can be done to alleviate the problem – when greater control can be exercised.[7] In many stressful situations the homosexual clergy are 'forced' into the use of less effective emotionally focused solutions because they perceive they have less control and fewer options open to them. This may have the effect of leading to greater emotional tension within the individual, less success in removing the problem, and subsequently greater feelings of helplessness in dealing with other problems that may arise. Homosexual clergy can be forced into a vicious cycle of greater self-doubt, more social withdrawal and increased emotional tension: 'doubt-out', as well as 'burnout'.

3. *Particular risks due to religious vocation.* Homosexuals are more likely to suffer from problems of identity, psychological isolation and societal pressures than heterosexuals but there are a number of reasons to predict that the situation will be much worse for the homosexual clergy. First, the Bible, by most reasonable interpretations, seems to present an ambiguous picture on the issue.[8] This may cause difficulties for the homosexual clergy because of inner doubts it raises in their minds. Heterosexual clergy do not have to face such deep questioning about their own sexuality because the biblical interpretations are usually focused on a discussion of whether or not they justify homosexuality.

It has been suggested that the Scriptures make many aspects of heterosexual behaviour suspect and that, in the extreme, 'the use of the Scriptures to condemn homosexuality – a tendency which exhibits many of the worst possible features of uncritical biblical exegesis – is still practised as a means of oppressing gay people'.[9] Thus, the homosexual clergyman or woman, whose whole life is based upon the Scriptures, is continually having to contend with interpretations of them which cast doubt on a central aspect of his or her being: his or her sexuality.

This is not all, of course. The homosexual clergyman may even question his very faith because for him God has made him homosexual in a heterosexual world. He may question his own morality and his own behaviour. He may be 'forced' into behaviours he is uncomfortable with because of insufficient channels for sexual release. He may question his 'weakness'. He may question his God. He may question his very being. Many heterosexuals have similar questions, but not generally with similar force, centrality or apparent reason. Clergy are, by definition, deeply religious people with particularly caring attitudes. It is likely, therefore, that homosexual clergy will be more greatly affected by religious uncertainties and personal questioning. It is rather interesting to note that celibacy is naturally accepted (and even applauded) as a gift from God to some (in the 1981 Synod debate on The Gloucester Report, Sister Carol says, 'I would not naturally have chosen celibacy; it was a gift of God towards me, a gift I sometimes find difficult to accept. One does not become a celibate overnight...'[10]). Homosexual priests would say the same about their homosexuality: not perverted but different.

The very vocation of the clergyman, however, may also require the homosexual clergyman to become a central figure in the lives of a community who share a different set of sexual and moral values. This is particularly likely in the case of the parish priest. The very focus of the job may require the vicar to take on roles and promote others which are at odds with his sexuality. This is a large area of potential inner conflict which is likely to push the clergyman into greater self-doubt and greater psychological isolation. The community focus of the job, which provides a great basis of support for the heterosexual clergyman, is one major source of stress for the homosexual clergyman: he does not 'fit' in important ways with the very fabric of his community. Of course, homosexual clergy learn to live with this. They have probably experienced the difficulties for some years, and they are used to being in a minority. These factors can, however, still have their silent costs for the psychological health of the minister and, because of the nature of his vocation, are likely to make him more vulnerable to illness than homosexuals in many other vocations. His job makes it much more difficult for him to 'come out' about his sexuality because most parishioners are likely to be unsympathetic and more hostile because he is the vicar; the bishop may well not accept the knowledge in a sympathetic enough manner, or he may not trust the bishop,[11] and the established Church position is somewhat negative.[12]

4. *Prejudice in the community*. It is probably true to say that there is a lack of sympathy towards homosexuals in the community at large, as well as a degree of prejudice about th·m. Homosexuals are often, for example, categorised on the basis of their sexuality in a way that heterosexuals are not.[13] The appearance of AIDS in the UK has reinforced ill-conceived views of homosexuals as being promiscuous carriers of pestilence from a God who is punishing Man for his sexual practices. It should be borne in mind that heterosexual AIDS presents the greatest growth curve in the USA at present and that in Africa it has spread mainly by heterosexual contact. There are undoubtedly promiscuous homosexual clergy, but they should not be considered to be representative of homosexual clergy. On the contrary, the homosexual clergy most likely to suffer from this public misconstrual are precisely those most different from the picture that is painted: the clergy in longstanding and permanent relationships analogous to marriage.

One result of community prejudice is that a great number of homosexuals, and a greater proportion of homosexual clergy, fear the consequences of being open with their family, friends, employers and others. Homosexuality can be hidden to a large extent, although this may itself have psychological costs, and in this sense is very different from other minority states. It is not usually, however, hidden out of choice: it is hidden because of community hostility.[14] This hostility, or at least the lack of understanding, is understandable but should not be condoned. I have to admit myself that while I have always professed no prejudice towards homosexuals I was uncertain and, to an extent, fearful about meeting the homosexual clergy discussed later in this chapter. I too had been taught inappropriate stereotypes. That is what prejudice is: judgement without knowledge. Prejudice is a kind of defensive mechanism for group identity and groups will try to preserve their own identity at the cost of others. The consequences of social pressure, however, are not just to cause inappropriate conformity; it also magnifies the difference for the individuals in the minority, causes them to cloister together, to become insular and therefore more prone to stress and burnout, and to defend themselves. This is unhealthy.

The problem of defining homosexuality and the prevalence of homosexual tendency

As yet there has been no attempt to define homosexuality in this book, nor any mention of how many clergymen in the Church of England are likely to be homosexual and, therefore, more prone to strain. These questions are, of course, interrelated.

Whatever definition is used, however, it seems that there are many more homosexuals in society than many people ordinarily suppose. For example, the American data from work done by Alfred Kinsey collected between 1938 and 1948, estimated that more than 4 per cent of US men aged 16–55 were exclusively homosexual throughout their lives, 10 per cent more or less exclusively homosexual for at least three years, and 37 per cent had 'overt homosexual sexual experience to the point of orgasm'.[15] These estimates, however, were based on very dubious methods which have been much criticised. New data were published in 1989, however, which countered many of the earlier problems. In an article by Fay, Turner, Klassen and Gagnon in the journal *Science*[16] *lower boundary* estimates of the prevalence of 'sexual contact to orgasm with another man' were made from surveys in 1970 and 1988. Overall, more than 20 per cent of the men had had homosexual experience, 8.8 per cent 'occasionally' or 'fairly often' and 6.7 per cent at the age of 20 or over. Considering just those men with a college education, whose backgrounds would be most similar to those of clergymen and ordinands, 31.8 per cent had some homosexual experience to orgasm, 8.3 per cent since they were 20 years old or more, and 4.2 per cent since they were older than 20 and where the frequency of such contact was at least 'occasional'. When discussing the results of estimates of those who admitted frequent homosexual behaviour, the authors concluded that the nature of the presumed reporting bias (that is, men not willing to admit to homosexuality), and the considerations of reasonable assumptions, 'indicates that the number might reasonable be estimated at almost twice this percentage'.[17] A recently reported study of the frequency of homosexual *intercourse* (presumed to be anal intercourse) by Forman and Chilvers[18] obtained a much lower percentage figure (1.17 per cent or 3 per cent with correction for under-reporting), but the figures involved were comparatively very small and the results at the lower end of the estimates by the Department of Health in 1988 which suggested that 3–7 per cent of the adult male population were homosexual.

All in all, these figures do support the view that a sizeable minority of the clergy of the Church of England are likely to be homosexual.

Two things are, however, difficult to estimate. First, it is unclear how many homosexual men will decide, or have decided, not to enter the Church because of the position held on the issue by it, or because of their interpretation of the Scriptures on this issue. Evidence suggests that this has not been too much of a bar in the past, but that the greater awareness of homosexuality at ordination may now be discouraging ordinands.[10] Second, it is not known whether the Church attracts a disproportionate number of homosexual males into its employ. Certainly more highly educated people are more likely to admit to being homosexual. It is also believed by some that the Church particularly attracts homosexual men, although in some cases this may be a response to concerns over sexuality; they may turn to God to resolve the inner worries this may cause. Obviously these two factors would work against each other in the effect they have on the numbers of homosexual clergy likely to be in full-time ministry. What will become clear just from clergy contacted in the research in this and the next chapter is that these numbers are not insignificant. We shall see whether they are significant in terms of their pastoral needs.

The essential questions with pastoral implications are whether or not homosexual clergy in the Church of England are more stressed than their heterosexual counterparts, whether they are strained in terms of the general population norms, whether many of them could be said to be strained at a 'case' level (that is, compared to those obtaining treatment from hospitals) and whether the strain levels they exhibit are a cause for concern.

Are homosexual clergy stressed?: the pilot study

A preliminary note about interpretation

When drawing conclusions from a sample of people about the total population from which they come, the representativeness of the sample is of paramount importance. When studying homosexual clergy it is very difficult indeed to know how representative one's sample is: have the methods used to contact them biased the sample? Does the nature of the investigations themselves minimise the likelihood of bias (for example, what about the ones who did not complete the questionnaire or interview)? Are the measures used actually measures of what you think they are? These are all important questions which dog social science research. The samples are never truly representative, however, the questions never quite right, and the methods never totally adequate.

What is important are the conclusions drawn on the basis of less than perfect evidence. This applies to the studies in this book, just as much as it does to any and every other study in which conclusions have to be drawn from evidence. It is tempting to put too much weight on these problems when the topic is controversial, or the findings difficult to come to terms with. When you are about to be critical of a study, say to yourself, 'Would I have been as critical had the results been different? Or if the topic had been a different one?' That does not mean asking the reader to remove all critical reasoning. What is needed is unbiased interpretation, and this probably requires greater critical faculty.

The pilot study sample

This small study was based on a questionnaire filled in by 40 male homosexual clergy who were all attending a clergy support group in England. No presumption is made that the sample are representative of homosexual clergy: they are almost certainly not, inasmuch as they had declared themselves sympathetic enough to attend a meeting for homosexual clergy, and had shown sufficient confidence to meet face-to-face with others. The support group has been in existence for some years and meets regularly, and so the meeting was not out of the ordinary. The clergy were from all parts of the country and their ages ranged from over 30 to mid-60s.

Each person filled in the Crown–Crisp Experiential Index, or Middlesex Hospital Questionnaire, some of the scales of which had been utilised in the study of parochial clergy outlined in the last chapter. The Index consists of 48 items and is a very well used and clinically validated instrument for which established norms exist.[20] It provides diagnostic information similar to that which may be gained from a formal clinical psychiatric or psychological examination in six different areas:

Free-floating anxiety (FFA): this is general anxiety without any specific focus or object for the anxiety (for example, feeling upset for no reason, feeling really panicky, feeling uneasy and restless).

Phobic anxiety (PHO): which is phobias of specific kinds (for example, of open spaces, crowds, enclosed spaces).

Obsessionality (OBS): which refers to things such as extreme meticulousness, excessive adherence to routines, and being a perfectionist.

Somatic anxiety (SOM): which refers to over-awareness or concern about bodily functions such as sweating, sleep disturbances and palpitations.

Depression (DEP): including sadness, feeling like crying, and feeling that life is too much effort.

Hysteria (HYS): which is similar to extroversion and refers to affectively labile individuals who have an over-dependence on other people.

The results from the 40 clergy are shown in Table 3.1. The table shows their mean score (each out of 16) and the percentage of clergy above a cut-off score indicating significant elevated levels for that condition. For purposes of comparison the table also presents the general population norms (for men aged 20–69 years old) for each scale and scores obtained from male psychoneurotic outpatients of a hospital.[21]

The scores of the homosexual clergy are clearly extremely high, which supports the view that they are suffering from high strain levels in terms of psychoneurotic and affective disorders. In fact, in total, 53 per cent of all the homosexual clergy in the pilot sample scored at or above the cut-off value on one or more of the four scales which can be considered to represent discrete categories of psychoneurotic illness (FFA, OBS, PHO and DEP). It is of great concern that one-third of the men were scoring at clinical 'case' levels on the anxiety scale.

Table 3.1 The psychological profiles of the homosexual pilot sample compared to norms.

| | Psychoneurotic or affective condition | | | | | |
	FFA	PHO	OBS	SOM	DEP	HYS
Homosexual clergy: Mean score (out of 16)	7.0	5.0	7.9	4.3	5.2	9.1
% above cut-off score*	33	20	28	18	13	78
Male general population norms	3.0	3.0	6.5	4.0	2.6	3.4
Psychoneurotic outpatient scores	9.7	5.3	8.7	8.0	7.7	5.2
(*Cut-off score used	10	0	11	9	9	7)

The clergy scored statistically higher than the male general population norms on five of the six sub-scales (the somaticism score did not differ). It will be noted from Table 3.1 that the clergy score particularly high on the hysteria sub-scale (9.1 compared to a norm of 3.4), with as many as 78 per cent of them scoring above the cut-off point. This may not be considered too surprising, given that the scale measures something not too dissimilar from extrovert personality, for individuals in such a 'people-orientated' profession. It is none the less a very high mean score and its significance is difficult to interpret. In other studies I have also shown that licensed taxi drivers in London and those learning to become taxi drivers ('Knowledge Boys/Girls') also have high scores on this hysteria scale which is probably due to the trade attracting extrovert people.[22] However, the mean score obtained for the taxi drivers, while high at 6.3, was significantly less than the 9.1 for the clergy in this pilot sample. The particularly elevated figure could be a characteristic or a consequence of being homosexual, a general feature of clergy, or an interaction of being both homosexual and being a priest. Previous research on the personality profiles of those ordained has suggested that one might expect clergy to be more obsessional, worrying, socially inept and even withdrawn than other individuals,[23] but this does not match the overall pattern found here.

Conclusions

There were a number of reasons to suppose that homosexual clergy might be a group particularly prone to the problems of stress. The results of the small pilot study seemed to support this view. The sample of 40 homosexual clergy who took part were found to be suffering from abnormal levels of strain. Indeed, the strain levels in that group were disturbingly high and, if in any sense representative of the situation within the Church of England, would pose a significant pastoral problem. Such levels of psychopathology have obvious implications for the personal well-being of the individuals concerned, but are also likely to represent considerable diminution in the functional ability of the clergy in their everyday work.

In order to investigate the problem in a more scientific manner it was considered necessary to complete a more thorough study on a much larger sample of homosexual clergy in the Church of England. It was considered necessary to attempt to ascertain more clearly whether the strain levels are high, what aspects of psychological and physical well-being might be compromised by stress, which aspects of the work itself contributed to the strain levels, and what contribution the particular stressors of being a homosexual priest made to the perception of work stress. This study is reported in the next chapter.

Notes

1. *Church of England Year Book*, 1989.
2. The Gloucester Report, paragraph 75, pp. 23–4.
3. Rich, Fowler, Young and Blenkush, 1986.
4. Babuscio, 1988, p. 5.
5. Ellis, Ames, Peckham and Burke, 1988.
6. Lazarus, 1966.
7. Folkman, 1984.
8. (See the Gloucester Report: *Homosexual Relationships*, 1979; Derrick Sherwin Bailey, *Homosexuality and the Western Christian Tradition*, 1955; John Boswell, *Christianity, Social Tolerance and Homosexuality*, 1981, for a discussion of the interpretation of the Scriptures.)
9. Babuscio, 1988, p. 82.
10. Proceedings of General Synod, 1981, p. 427.
11. See the case study in Chapter 5.
12. See Chapter 6.
13. See the case study in Chapter 5.
14. See Babuscio, 1988.
15. Kinsey, Pomeroy and Martin, 1949, p. 650.
16. Fay *et al.*, 1989.
17. *Ibid.*, p. 347.
18. Forman and Chilvers, 1989.
19. See the ACCM figures.
20. Crown and Crisp, 1979.
21. Both taken from Crown and Crisp, 1979. It will be noted that the cut-off scores used for each sub-scale are greater than the mean outpatient scores since they are based on dysfunction-specific clinical norms where possible (primarily from people suffering from depression, free-floating anxiety, phobic anxiety or obsessionality).
22. Fletcher and Morris, 1989.
23. Dunn, 1965.

4
Stress among Homosexual Clergy: the Principal Study

The major questions to be answered in this chapter are:

1. Are homosexual clergy under significant levels of strain, as measured by valid barometers of psychological health? We saw in Chapter 2 that parochial clergy perceived themselves as under a number of psychological pressures, although the overall level of psychopathology was relatively good. Are the levels of strain higher among homosexual than heterosexual clergy? The pilot study reported in Chapter 3 would suggest this is so.

2. What physical manifestations of stress do homosexual clergy suffer from?

3. Are homosexual clergy under more stress than heterosexual clergy?

4. What are the possible causes of strain among homosexual clergy? Are the effects of their sexuality of primary importance in how they perceive the demands of the job? Which work stressors are associated with the strain levels?

5. Do such factors as sexual frustration and sexual drive affect strain levels, or do they mediate the effects of the work and sexuality demands on strain?

6. What aspects of their life do homosexual clergy find supportive, and do these perceived supports actually have any effects on lowering strain

levels? We saw in Chapter 2 that support factors did not appear to play much of a role in reducing strain in the parochial clergy.

7. Do clergy in different types of job (for example, incumbents, team vicars, curates, chaplains) show different levels of stressors and strains?

8. Are there differences in stressors and strain levels in different types of parish location? One might expect, for example, that homosexual clergy in rural locations would show higher strain levels because they are more likely to suffer from the stressors detailed in Chapter 3 (for example, they have less opportunity for social support).

9. How many homosexual clergy are there in the Church of England, and how big, therefore, is the resulting stress problem? If the results of the pilot study were confirmed to any extent, and if there is a significant minority of clergy who are homosexual, the Church of England would need seriously to consider the pastoral implications with some urgency.

To answer these questions a study was designed and executed in the early part of 1989. The homosexual clergy were contacted, by post, through necessarily clandestine routes, although all had 'come out' to the extent of belonging to clergy groups which exist for the specific purpose of mutual identification and support. The groups meet on a regular but infrequent basis almost exclusively to discuss topics of religious import. Although I did not meet many of the clergy face-to-face, they were informed about the study by a prior letter from the organiser of the support networks who asked for their co-operation. The study sample consisted of 390 homosexual clergy; they were asked to complete the questionnaire only if they were definitely homosexual.

The questionnaries, to be completed anonymously, were sent out during February and March 1989. They were sent together with a prepaid addressed label for return to me at Hatfield Polytechnic. The response rate was somewhat disappointing at 44 per cent. Although this figure is very high indeed for a postal questionnaire of this nature, it will be recalled that the return rate in the study of parochial clergy was 62 per cent. The relatively low response rate is understandable and can probably be attributed to three factors. First, the questionnaires came from, and had to be returned to, an outside agent (that is, myself) of whom the clergy in question knew relatively little. Second, given the considerable concerns most homosexual clergy have of being 'found out', many were probably reluctant to put anything down on paper (some of the completed questionnaires contained no handwriting at all) and return it in an envelope which would be postmarked. Third, the questionnaire did ask the respondents to reveal quite personal details about such things as their living arrangements and their sexual frustrations, as well as their perceptions of work and other matters.

One question to be addressed immediately is how representative the sample was of homosexual clergy in the Church of England. Since the names of the respondents were not recorded on the questionnaires, no follow-up of non-respondents was possible. It is also true that the respondents were part of the clergy support group network, and it is difficult to know if this makes them more or less likely to show higher strain levels, or whether only the most (or least) stressed individuals bothered to complete and return the questionnaires. On the one hand it could be argued that those in the sample are likely to be less stressed than homosexual clergy in general because they have 'come out', albeit to a minor degree, by belonging to the groups. It has been suggested[1] that such 'belonging' is a basic emotional human need and that homosexuals who do not identify with others of like sexuality will be more prone to psychological problems. On the other hand, one could interpret the belonging more as a cry for help from more greatly stressed individuals. While there seems little doubt that the support groups do indeed provide psychological support, it would be my judgement that their members are *less* likely to be suffering from strain. There are a number of reasons for thinking this. The vast majority of those belonging to the support groups contacted could be described as Liberal-Catholics, or of the Liberal-Catholic centre, in terms of churchmanship, and this itself will be a support. Those priests of Anglo-Catholic tradition who look to Rome are much more likely to be stressed because their sexuality is fundamentally at odds with their churchmanship and they are likely to have strongly to oppose any homosexual sympathies in public, to themselves, and to many other clergy. The case discussed in Chapter 6 below[2] could be considered as a possible demonstration of the consequences of a person's understanding of sexuality being at odds with churchmanship. It may also be a salutary lesson for the Church of England in what may happen if the homosexuality issue is not positively considered from a pastoral perspective. Those homosexuals of the Evangelical tradition, too, would also be more likely to be stressed because of the inner tension between their views on the Scriptures and their sexuality: their whole perspective on the Scriptures would make it harder for them to accept their sexuality. In conclusion, then, it is suggested that the sample of homosexual clergy who formed the basis for this study are not likely to over-represent the stress problem.

What is much more difficult to estimate is the proportion of the Church of England clergy who are homosexual. One can only guesstimate. Informed workers in this area believe that for every one person contacted for the survey there are two to three other clergy who are homosexual. This must be considered a conservative estimate,[3] and would result in a figure of around 1,400 homosexual clergy. This would imply that a far larger proportion of clergy in the Church of England are homosexual compared to population norms for those with college education.[4] This is understandable, for a number of reasons. First, the Church is one of the caring professions, and provides the homosexual, who, *in general*, would not have children or get married, with a channel for parental instincts of caring. Some years ago, the Church was one of the few professions where this was possible (social work, for example, was not an option). Second, the reports of homosexuals[5] suggest that being homosexual results in many and various forms of subtle and explicit emotional persecution from an early age, which may in turn develop into greater concern for those in a vulnerable position. Third, some may turn towards the spiritual and religious in an attempt to understand their sexuality, or to channel their frustrated sexual energies.

For purposes of comparison, the strain levels of the homosexual clergy were compared to those obtained from the study of parochial clergy outlined in Chapter 2. The major purpose of this comparison was to attempt to determine if homosexual clergy were under higher or lower levels of stress than heterosexual clergy. The age profiles of the two samples, however, did differ slightly: the parochial clergy sample had a higher proportion of clergy aged over 60, and a lower proportion of those under 40. Although age showed no statistical associations with depression and anxiety levels in the parochial clergy it was still decided to match the age profiles of both samples as far as was possible. As a consequence of this, some of the figures given in this chapter may be slightly different from those in Chapter 2. There is another problem in using the parochial clergy as a heterosexual control group. It was never intended originally to compare the groups in this manner and it is almost certain that a proportion of the parochial clergy were also homosexual since they were a random sample of clergy on full-time stipends in the Church of England. The only check on their sexuality was that the names picked from *Crockford's* did not include those whose names were identified as belonging to the sample of homosexual clergy. From some of the spontaneous comments made by the parochial clergy it was clear that a number were homosexual and it is likely, given the estimates above, that a fair minority of the 'heterosexual' clergy were unidentified homosexuals. This is not a serious problem for the major purposes of the study because any differences in the stress levels of the two groups will be attenuated if homosexual clergy are more stressed than heterosexual clergy.

A final point needs to be reiterated before presenting the study itself. It is of considerable significance whether or not the homosexual clergy are *practising* homosexuals. The Church may well feel that, in the majority of cases, this is not so. It should be noted that, *for the purposes of determining caring strategies*, the answer to this question is largely irrelevant. If homosexual clergy are under high levels of strain there is a pastoral need whether or not they are 'practising'. The clergy were not asked this question since it is difficult to define what one means by 'practising', and because it was not central to the major topic under investigation. Since the study was completed, however, I have done some research on the topic by questioning a number of homosexual clergy about their own perceptions of what is generally the case. Their responses have been unambiguous: many priests will say they are not practising homosexuals, to protect themselves; if they are committed to someone it would be unusual for them not to engage in sexual activity;[6] and they have no doubt that the majority of clergy who took part in the study are likely to be practising homosexuals.

The questionnaires

The questionnaire was designed to be almost completely made up of multiple-choice questions. It consisted of 96 questions in six different sections:

1. **Background details**, including age, sex, marital status, stipendiary type, parish location, whether or not they were living with a same-sex partner, and level of job satisfaction.

2. **General work demands**. This consisted of 15 items, which had to be assessed in terms of demandingness (using the same 1–5 scale, with a '0', or not relevant, category, detailed in the job demands section of the parochial clergy study).

3. **Sexuality and work demands**, which had 11 items, to assess the way in which the effects of being homosexual influenced the demandingness of their work. The response scale was the same as that in Section 2.

4. **Job supports**, consisting of 15 items, which assessed the degree of perceived support available to the clergy to meet the effects of the demands they were placed under. The response scale was identical to that used in the comparable section of the parochial clergy study.

5. **Medical and sexual information** had 12 questions, which asked about smoking and drinking habits, height and weight, physical and psychological manifestations of stress, sexual drive and sexual frustration.

6. **Psychological health and well-being**, which consisted of 24 questions from the Crown–Crisp Experiential Index used in the study of parochial clergy, measuring free-floating anxiety, depression and somatic anxiety, and a 12-item 'Thoughts & Feelings' questionnaire taken from Fletcher's Occupational Stress Audit/Cultural Audit[7] which contains items to measure general anxiety, depression and somaticism.

Results: Background information

Age and sex

The great majority of the homosexual clergy were male (99 per cent). Their average age was 45 years and 6 months, with 35 per cent under 40, 28 per cent 40–49, 25 per cent 50–59, and 10 per cent over 60 years old.

Partnership status

Twenty-five per cent of the clergy said they lived with their same-sex partner, which is a surprisingly large figure, given the obvious difficulties this must present for the priest. It does suggest that at least a significant minority of the clergy are in long-term relationships from which they may gain considerable support. Not surprisingly, the majority were single (89 per cent), with 7 per cent being married, 2 per cent widowed and only one individual divorced. The fact that most are single shows that most have not opted for the 'halo of marriage'. Given the age profile of the clergy, however, the fact that they are single makes them somewhat conspicuous, as well as creating suspicions of heterosexual single clergy. This may have particular relevance at the time of selection of ordinands, or at ordination.

Type of stipend

The majority of the sample were parochial clergy: 51 per cent were incumbents, 11 per cent were team vicars/priests, 12 per cent curates and 8 per cent chaplains, with the remainder holding other posts (including monks, cathedral clergy and synod staff).

Type of parish

Fourteen per cent reported that their parish was primarily rural, 18 per cent suburban, 36 per cent from the dioceses of London/Southwark, and 25 per cent from other urban areas. There is clearly a geographic bias in the sample, since the dioceses of London and Southwark contain something less than 10 per cent of the stipendiary clergy, according to Church statistics. This bias may reflect a true geographical distribution of homosexual clergy, who might be expected to gravitate towards the capital, where they would not be in such a small minority, and their sexuality would consequently be more easily hidden from others. On the other hand, it may be that the support group structure, which formed the means of contacting the clergy, is better developed in the capital, and would, therefore, be responsible for their over-representation.

Estimation of percentage of homosexual clergy in the Church of England

If the dioceses of London and Southwark do represent the situation for the provinces of Canterbury and York, the proportion of homosexual clergy in the Church of England *who are also part of the homosexual clergy support groups* would be estimated at 14 per cent (59 clergy taken as 44 per cent [survey response rate] were from London and Southwark which contains about 976 stipendiary clergy).[8] Even though these dioceses do probably contain a higher proportion of homosexual clergy than exists in other parts of the country, it should be reiterated that this estimate is based on homosexual clergy who belong to a support group. It would seem that my previous estimates, based on discussions with reliable and informed sources, which suggested that around 15 per cent of Church of England clergy are homosexual, is not an overestimate. It must be clear from these estimates that homosexual clergy do form a very significant proportion of Church of England clergy, and should be considered an important section.

Smoking, drinking, weight and height

The average weight of the clergy was 167 lb (11 stone 13 lb) with a range of 8 stone 4 lb to 16 stone 8 lb. Average height was 5 ft 10 in with a range of 5 ft 1 in to 6 ft 5 in.

Only 16 per cent said they smoked regularly, with 5 per cent smoking 1–10 cigarettes a day, 5 per cent 11–20, 5 per cent 21–30 and 1 per cent over 30. Thus the clergy are less likely to smoke, and consume fewer cigarettes, than the general population.

Some 78 per cent of the respondents said they drank alcohol regularly, although the majority (56 per cent) had two or less units a day. Only one individual admitted to drinking in excess of nine units daily, with 4 per cent having 6–8, and 18 per cent 3–5 units/day.

Job satisfaction

Job satisfaction was measured by a single item, ('*Overall*, how satisfied are you with your job?') which asked clergy to place a cross on a 7-point scale with .1 representing 'extremely dissatisfied' and 7 'extremely satisfied'. The mean job satisfaction score of the respondents was 5, which shows that overall the clergy were quite satisfied with their jobs. Only 1 per cent of the clergy were 'extremely dissatisfied', 6 per cent scored 2 and 7 per cent scored 3. Twelve per cent were neither satisfied nor dissatisfied, 33 per cent scored 5, 35 per cent scored 6 and 6 per cent scored 7. These results are relatively encouraging and show the homosexual clergy to be quite happy in their work.

Table 4.1 shows the job satisfaction scores according to parish type and type of stipend. The table indicates (and this was confirmed statistically) that rural clergy and curates tend to be less satisfied than the other comparative groups. This is also reflected in the percentages in each group who were 'extremely satisfied' with their job: no curates, or those in rural locations, gave such a rating. The team vicars/priests-in-charge from suburban parishes also had particularly low job satisfaction (the mean score for the six people in this category was only 3.5).

Table 4.1 Job satisfaction according to type of stipend and parish location.

Job satisfaction scale: 1–7; 1 = extremely dissatisfied, 7 = extremely satisfied

	Mean score	% scoring 6	% scoring 7
Whole sample	5.0	35	6
Parish location			
Rural	4.5	18	0
Suburban	4.8	31	7
London/Southwark	4.9	36	3
Other urban	5.2	39	10
Stipendiary type			
Incumbent	5.1	39	4
Team vicar	4.9	39	6
Curate	4.5	21	0
Others	4.8	30	12

Strain indicators

There were two main scales measuring strain levels (that is, the effects of stress):the Crown–Crisp Experiential Index [CCEI] and the Thoughts and Feelings Questionnaire [TFQ]. In addition, respondents were asked if they had felt as though they were going to have a nervous breakdown in the past year, and how, if relevant, they had found stress manifesting itself in terms of physical illnesses.

Nervous breakdown feelings

A rather large proportion of the homosexual clergy (26 per cent) said they had felt as though they were going to have a nervous breakdown within the previous year, with the remaining 74 per cent saying they had not had this feeling. This is a very high percentage indeed. The tendency to have felt this was affected by the age of the respondent, with younger respondents being more likely to affirm it.

The likelihood of clergy having felt as though they were going to have a nervous breakdown in the preceding year was not affected by whether or not the clergy lived with their same-sex partner, although both type of stipendiary and type of parish did show variations (bearing in mind the relatively small numbers in some categories). Only 19 per cent of incumbents reported having had the feeling, compared to 44 per cent of team vicars/priests-in-charge, and 32 per cent of curates. The 'other stipend' categories produced a figure of 28 per cent. As many as 36 per cent of clergy in rural locations reported they had had the feeling, compared to 25 per cent in the dioceses of London/Southwark, 24 per cent in other urban areas, and 21 per cent in suburban areas.

Clergy reporting higher levels of job satisfaction were also less likely to have felt as though they were going to have a nervous breakdown.[9]

Stress and physical health

The clergy were asked: 'In the past year if you have been suffering from stress has it been manifesting itself in physical illness?' In response to this 28 per cent ticked the 'not applicable' box, that is, they had not suffered from stress. Fifty-one per cent ticked the 'Yes' category, although the most commonly reported manifestation of physical 'illness' was 'tiredness', which was generated by 21 per cent of those in this category. Of the other frequent manifestations listed by the clergy, cardiovascular problems, for example, hypertension, myocardial infarction, arrhythmias, were mentioned by 14 per cent, eczema and rashes by 14 per cent, migraine and headache by 14 per cent, colds, flu and other minor infections by 14 per cent, insomnia by 12 per cent, back trouble/pain by 9 per cent, asthma by 4 per cent, and diarrhoea by 4 per cent. Other manifestations listed included AIDS, attacks of aphasia, and post-viral fatigue syndrome. Of the 22 per cent who ticked the 'No' category the majority of manifestations centred on tiredness and lethargy, panic feelings, depression and irritability.

Psychological well-being

In this section there were measures of free-floating or general anxiety, depression and somatic anxiety. The major comparisons to be made are:

1. The difference, if any, between the strain levels of homosexual clergy and of the parochial clergy reported in Chapter 2.

2. The difference, if any, between the strain levels of homosexual clergy and men of comparable age and social class in the general population.[10]

3. The percentage of homosexual clergy with definite psychopathology.[11]

Free-floating or general anxiety

The homosexual clergy were significantly more stressed than the heterosexual parochial clergy in terms of the mean score on the comparable anxiety scale. The mean score of the homosexual clergy on the anxiety scale of the CCEI was 5.3, which is statistically significantly more than the general population mean for men aged 45–54 of 3.2.

Over 15 per cent of the homosexual clergy scored at case levels of free-floating anxiety (that is, they scored more than those suffering from clinical anxiety according to the norms). Only 2 per cent of the heterosexual clergy had comparable high scores. On the 'thoughts and feelings' general anxiety scale 19 per cent scored more than 12, out of a maximum of 16, suggesting very high levels of anxiety. Table 4.2 presents the pattern of responses of the homosexual clergy on the TFQ anxiety items. It can be seen, for example, that 27 per cent of them said they 'very frequently/often' felt 'constant worrying causing a feeling of tension'.

Depression

The homosexual clergy scored significantly higher than the heterosexual clergy on the depression scales. For the homosexual clergy the mean depression score on the CCEI scale was 5.8, compared to 3.1 for the comparable male general population. This difference is statistically highly significant. A large number of homosexual clergy could be described as depressed at a case level. Twenty per cent of them scored at least as high as clinically depressed individuals,[12] while only 5 per cent of the parochial clergy sample in Chapter 2 scored similarly high. On the 'thoughts and feelings' depression scale, 20 per cent scored more than 12, which indicates a high level of depressive thoughts among the sample. For example, 17 per cent of the homosexual clergy very frequently or often felt low and wanted to give up trying (see Table 4.2).

Table 4.2 The pattern of responses of homosexual clergy on the thoughts and feelings questionnaire

	% reporting feeling: very frequently	never
General anxiety items		
Constant worrying causing a feeling of tension	27	10
Finding it difficult to think on the spot/concentrate on one thing at a time	12	11
Feeling like 'falling apart at the seams' without knowing why	7	43
Feeling ill at ease and needing to escape	13	23
Depression items		
Feelings of sadness on awakening	17	18
Feeling low and wanting to give up	10	20
Loss of interest in going out and socialising	14	16
Having difficulty coping with the problems of living	9	22

Somatic anxiety

The homosexual clergy also scored significantly higher than the heterosexual parochial clergy on the somatic anxiety scales, although neither group showed significantly elevated scores, and the mean for the homosexual clergy was not different from the male population norms. Six per cent of the homosexual clergy did score at least as high as psychoneurotic outpatients,[13] although none of the heterosexual clergy did. One of the somaticism items on the TFQ is concerned with feeling exhausted and having little physical stamina and 24 per cent reported having this feeling very frequently. This corresponds closely to the 21 per cent who reported tiredness as a manifestation of their stress problems (see the 'Stress and physical health' section above).

Strain levels, parish location and type of stipend

Table 4.3 presents a picture of the percentage of homosexual clergy who score sufficiently highly on the TFQ scales to be considered as showing disabling psychological dysfunction for each stipendiary type and parish location. A number of aspects are worth commenting on. First, more clergy in rural locations and urban locations outside London show such high scores. A similar picture was present in the CCEI scores.

The pattern for the rural locations is the opposite of what one would expect to find from population norms, where those from rural locations usually have lower scores on such scales,[14] and suggests that the situation of homosexual rural clergy is particularly problematic. The second aspect of the figures worth commenting upon is that the homosexual clergy within the London and Southwark Dioceses do not score highly *relative to other parish locations*. Thus the relatively large proportion of clergy from these dioceses is not responsible for the generally high levels of strain observed in the sample as a whole. Third, team vicars/priests-in-charge and curates are the personnel associated with the highest levels of strain. In fact 32 per cent of the curates scored at case level on the free-floating anxiety scale of the CCEI.

Table 4.3 Psychopathology of homosexual clergy according to parish location and type of stipend (% scoring at disabling or case level)

| | TFQ scale: | | |
	anxiety	depression	somaticism
Parish location			
Rural	23%	23%	4%
Suburban	21%	17%	0%
London/Southwark	14%	14%	3%
Other urban	22%	31%	0%
Stipendiary type			
Incumbent	17%	20%	1%
Team vicar/priest-in-charge	22%	22%	0%
Curate	26%	21%	5%
Other stipends	16%	19%	2%

Although the somaticism levels of the clergy were not high (in fact they were particularly low for 'other stipends' in rural locations) the incumbents in rural parishes showed the highest levels of somatic anxiety.

Work demands

To measure work demands, respondents had to assess each of 15 statements in terms of how much they agreed or disagreed that these factors made their job more difficult or demanding. They used a 5-point scale, on which 5 represented the highest demand. If a particular work factor was not relevant to their situation they were asked to respond with a 0.

Table 4.4 Job demand ratings of the homosexual clergy

	Mean score	%5 rating	%0 rating
Job requires more work than time available to do it in	4.0	36	1
Sheer load of work	3.8	25	1
Demands of individual parishioners	3.7	14	11
Playing such a major role in the lives of those in the community	3.6	14	6
Pressures of continually creating new ideas and solving problems	3.6	13	3
Having continually to 'put on a public face'	3.5	20	1
Working alone or in comparative isolation	3.5	15	14
Lack of clear division between work and home making job demanding	3.5	17	7
Dealing with important aspects of lives of others (e.g. funerals, marriages)	3.4	11	7
Insufficient financial resources make job demanding	3.3	11	9
Lack of interest of parishioners	3.1	9	14
Having to talk in public	2.8	7	3
Having an unclear role	2.6	7	4
Factors at home making job demanding	2.4	3	13
Being unsure about faith makes job demanding	2.1	2	4

The results of interest include the mean levels of job demand for each item, excluding the 0 or 'not relevant' scores, the percentage of clergy who rate each work factor as highly demanding with a score of 5, the number for whom an item was not considered relevant, and whether or not the work demands were correlated with the strain measures, that is, depression, anxiety, somaticism.

Total work demands

An overall work demands score was obtained by summing the scores for all the 15 demand items. For the homosexual clergy this mean total was 45.6 which corresponds to an average rating of just over 3 for each item. The minimum score for any priest was 17, that is, an average of only 1.1 for each item, and the highest score 67, that is, an average 4.5.

It was found that the higher the overall work demands the higher levels of general anxiety, depression and somaticism, as shown by the statistical correlations between the total work demand scores and each of the strain scales.[15] Higher total work demand was also associated with lower job satisfaction.[16] The likelihood of a cleric having felt as though he was going to have a nervous breakdown in the previous year was also greater if the perceived level of work demands was greater.[17]

Specific work demands

Although the previous section showed that the total work demands had an effect on the well-being of the homosexual clergy, it is useful to try to determine which particular aspects of work are most likely to cause lowered psychological health. This section shows the work factors the clergy perceived as most demanding, and also which were associated with poorer well-being (since it is not always the case that what people think is stressing them actually is). Table 4.4 presents the work demands in rank order according to perceived demandingness (the mean scores), followed by the number of clergy who rated each in the 5 (very demanding) category, and the number for whom it was rated 0 or 'not relevant'. Mean demand scores are calculated with the 'not relevant' ratings excluded.

Table 4.4 gives something of a 'demandingness' description of the job, and it is interesting to note that, as with the parochial clergy sample, the overall workload is perceived as being problematic. This is probably contrary to the expectations of members of the public who do not understand the many facets of the clerics' jobs. It is relevant to note that a number of the items were given a 5 rating by more than 10 per cent of the clergy. The 20 per cent who found 'having to continually put on a public face' very demanding may have been referring to this in relation to their homosexuality. The fact that only 2 per cent found issues of faith making their job difficult does suggest that the homosexual clergy do not, in general, have concerns about their religious beliefs.

Table 4.5 provides a picture of the relationship between psychological health[18] and the demands which appeared in Table 4.4. Only those demands which showed a statistically significant association are shown.

It can be seen from Table 4.5 that most of the aspects of demand were associated with poorer psychological health, in terms of depression, anxiety and somaticism. The size of the associations, while somewhat modest, are all in the predicted direction: higher demand with higher strain. The demand ranked first in Table 4.4 (lack of time) was not predictive of strain levels, nor was having to deal with important aspects of the lives of others, or having to talk in public.

Table 4.5 Job demands related to poorer psychological health (anxiety [ANX], depression [DEP] and somaticism [SOM]: ns = not significant)

	ANX	DEP	SOM
Sheer load of work	0.20	0.15	0.17
Demands of individual parishioners	0.22	0.16	0.24
Playing such a major role in the lives of those in the community	0.22	0.18	0.14
Pressures of continually creating new ideas and solving problems	0.20	0.20	0.19
Having continually to 'put on a public face'	0.28	0.29	0.21
Working alone or in comparative isolation	0.27	0.25	0.14
Lack of clear division between work and home making job demanding	0.18	0.23	0.26
Insufficient financial resources makes job demanding	ns	0.14	ns
Lack of interest of parishioners	0.17	0.16	0.13
Having an unclear role	0.31	0.27	0.18
Factors at home making job demanding	0.17	0.14	ns
Being unsure about faith makes job demanding	0.18	0.28	ns

Job satisfaction and specific demands

Job satisfaction appeared to be affected by some of the specific job demands. Individuals who were: (a) less sure of their faith, (b) less clear about their role, (c) find their parishioners' lack of interest demanding, (d) find working in comparative isolation demanding, or (e) who have demanding individuals in their parish, were likely to show lower job satisfaction scores.[19]

Specific job demands and type of stipend

Of course, the precise demands made on a priest will also be determined by the job he does: one might expect an incumbent, for example, to be more concerned than some other stipendairy types about demands relating to parishioners. Table 4.6 presents the data on each specific work-demand for each of the stipendiary types separately. In this, and subsequent tables of this kind, the mean scores have been calculated with the 0 or 'not relevant' reponses included.

Table 4.6 Job demand profiles for each stipendiary type (mean demand scores)

Job demand	Incumbent	Team vicar/priest-in-charge	Curate	Other
Lack of time	4.0	4.1	3.8	3.6
Sheer load of work	3.7	3.8	3.3	3.8
Individual parishioners	3.6	3.8	3.5	2.4
Major role in lives	3.5	3.0	3.8	3.2
Creativity/problem solving	3.4	3.7	3.3	3.4
'Public face'	3./	2.8	3.8	3.3
Isolation	3.2	3.1	3.1	2.6
Work/home blur	3.5	3.3	3.7	2.4
Funerals, marriages, etc.	3.5	2.9	3.0	2.7
Finances	3.3	3.3	3.0	2.4
Parishioners' lack of interest	3.0	2.9	3.2	1.6
Public talking	2.6	2.8	2.3	3.1
Unclear role	2.3	2.4	3.0	2.5
Home	2.0	2.4	1.9	2.2
Unsure faith	2.0	1.9	1.9	2.0

Specific work demands and location of parish

Table 4.7 presents the effects of each work demand of the location or type of parish in which the priest works.

Table 4.7 Job demands for each of the types of parish

Job demand	Rural	Suburban	London/Southwark	Other urban
Lack of time	4.0	3.9	3.9	3.9
Sheer load of work	3.5	3.7	3.6	3.9
Individual parishioners	3.5	3.6	3.0	3.5
Major role in lives	3.6	3.5	3.3	3.3
Creativity/problem solving	3.8	3.6	3.5	3.0
'Public face'	3.9	3.7	3.4	3.4
Isolation	3.7	3.5	2.6	3.0
Work/home blur	3.4	3.7	3.2	3.3
Funerals, marriages, etc.	3.6	3.0	3.1	3.3
Finances	2.7	3.0	3.3	3.1
Parishioners' lack of interest	3.1	2.9	2.6	2.6
Public talking	3.3	2.8	2.5	2.7
Unclear role	2.5	2.7	2.6	2.2
Home	2.1	1.9	2.3	2.0
Unsure faith	2.2	1.9	2.1	1.8

Overall, it will be seen from Tables 4.6 and 4.7 that there are a number of differences between how the demands are perceived, depending upon where the clergy live and what category of stipend they belong to.

Sexuality and work demands

Eleven items referred to possible work demands which may arise from being a homosexual cleric. The same rating scale as 'work demands' (above) was used.

Table 4.8 Sexuality demands experienced by the homosexual clergy

Sexuality demand item	Mean score	% 5 rating	% 0
The 'established church view' on sexuality (e.g. General Synod) making the job demanding	4.2	42	1
General hostility within the community at large	3.8	24	3
Worrying about the media (e.g. press) finding out about their homosexuality	3.7	32	1
Promotions within the Church more unlikely because of homosexuality	3.7	27	6
Job difficult because dealing with parishioners with traditional views on sexuality	3.6	14	3
Demands of not being open with parishioners about homosexuality	3.6	17	7
Being a minority group in the Church of England	3.5	14	5
Having to conceal homosexuality from other priests	3.0	6	11
Espousing views in public at odds with their sexuality	3.0	9	4
Concealing homosexuality from wife/family/children	3.0	3	59
Not being open with the bishop makes job demanding	2.9	6	15

Total sexuality demands

The average total sexuality demands score (that is, the total score for the 11 items) was related to each of the strain scales. For example, the higher the sexuality score obtained, the higher the levels of strain on all the 'thoughts and feelings' scales.[20]

Total sexuality demand score also varied significantly with type of stipend and location of parish: incumbents and curates scored more highly than both team vicars/priests-in-charge and 'other stipends'; and clergy in the rural or suburban locations scored more highly than those in urban locations (including London and Southwark dioceses).

Table 4.8 presents the overall picture of sexuality demands experienced by the clergy. It will be noted that 'the established Church of England views on homosexuality' are ranked as the most important perceived sexuality demand. This item proved to be the single most important demand of all the 26 work and sexuality demand items measured.

Sex demands and psychological health

Six of the sexuality demands were associated with psychological ill-health. Community hostility, parishioners' traditionalism, having to conceal sexuality from parishioners, from wife/children/family, being in a minority group in the Church of England, and having to espouse views at odds with sexuality, each showed significant statistical correlations with the three TFQ scales of general anxiety, depression and somaticism. It is notable that some of the sexuality demands which were ranked as most important by the clergy (for example, the Church of England views on homosexuality) were not associated with lower psychological health. This suggests that although such matters are in the forefront of their minds, they do not significantly affect psychological health.

Sex demands and job satisfaction

Three sex demands were significantly and negatively correlated with job satisfaction, showing that higher demands were associated with lower job satisfaction: not being open with parishioners about homosexuality; having to conceal sexuality from family, etc.; and the general community hostility to homosexuals.[21]

Sexuality demands and stipend type

Table 4.9 presents the data for each sex demand (and total sexuality demand) according to stipendiary type.

Table 4.9 Sexuality demands according to stipend

Sexuality demand	Incumbent	Team vicar/ priest-in-charge	Curate	Other clergy
Established Church views	4.1	4.1	4.4	4.1
Community hostility	3.8	3.3	4.2	3.9
Media worry	3.9	3.2	3.9	3.4
Prejudice promotions	3.6	3.3	3.6	3.2
Parishioners' traditionalism	3.6	3.5	3.9	3.2
Conceal from parishioners	3.6	3.0	3.9	2.5
C of E minority group	3.6	3.1	3.7	3.5
Conceal from priests	2.9	2.3	2.8	2.2
Espousing conflicting views	3.1	2.3	3.3	2.5
Conceal from wife/family/children	1.5	1.5	0.7	0.7
Conceal from bishop	2.6	2.2	2.6	2.2
Total sexuality demands	36.4	31.8	37.1	31.5

Specific sexuality demands and location of parish

Table 4.10 shows the mean sexuality demand scores for each separate item for each of the parish location types.

Table 4.10 Sexuality demands according to parish location

Sexuality demand	Rural	Suburban	London/ Southwark	Other urban
Established Church views	4.4	4.1	4.1	4.0
Community hostility	4.1	3.9	3.6	3.9
Media worry	4.2	3.8	3.6	3.5
Prejudice promotions	3.3	3.6	3.6	3.4
Parishioners' traditionalism	4.2	3.9	3.2	3.4
Conceal from parishioners	3.8	3.8	3.3	3.0
C of E minority group	3.8	3.6	3.6	3.4
Conceal from priests	3.3	3.1	2.4	2.7
Espousing conflicting views	3.4	3.2	2.7	2.9
Conceal from wife/family/children	1.8	1.2	1.2	1.1
Conceal from bishop	2.6	3.2	2.2	2.4
Total sexuality demands	38.9	37.4	33.5	33.7

Factors which provide support

There were 15 items relevant to potential supports, and clergy were required to rate them on a scale of how much it made their job easier (5 = 'My job is always made much easier by it/them') or harder (1 = job always made harder by it/them). Again a 0 response was provided to indicate the factor was 'not relevant' to them. These 0 responses were not included in calculations of mean support scores.

Total job support

A mean total support score obtained by adding the responses to each of the 15 items was calculated for each clergyman, and this was compared to their levels of psychological health on each of the strain scales. The higher this total support score, the lower the level of depression;[22] and the higher the support, the greater the job satisfaction.[23] Team vicars/priests-in-charge from rural parishes had particularly high levels of support, while the 'other stipends' from rural locations showed the lowest levels of overall support.

Specific work supports

Table 4.11 presents a picture of which particular factors clergy found most and least supportive.

Table 4.11 Support factors for homosexual clergy

	Mean score	% 5 rating	% 0
Support item			
Freedom to do things considered important	4.2	39	5
Support from non-religious friends	4.2	36	6
Religious beliefs and strength from God	4.1	37	1
Seeing the results of work	4.1	28	4
Support from other local homosexual clergy	4.1	24	23
Support from spouse/family	4.0	16	53
Encouragement from parishioners	3.9	22	13
Support from homosexual clergy support groups	3.9	17	21
The intellectual challenge of their ministry	3.8	19	8
Providing an important service to the community	3.7	15	6
Knowing they are part of a caring profession	3.6	15	12
Support from local heterosexual clergy	3.6	8	11
Encouragement and support from bishop	3.4	10	17
Thoroughness of training for the priesthood	3.3	12	11
Clarity of mission	3.3	10	6

It will be noted that many of the homosexual clergy find considerable support from their religious beliefs and strength from God, although job autonomy and support from non-religious friends are most important. There were a number of significant effects of these support factors on psychological health. The greater the perceived support from religious beliefs, the lower the scores on each of three scales of psychological health in the TFQ. A similar pattern was present for the support from being part of a caring profession, and providing an important service to the community.

Specific support items and job satisfaction

Seven of the support items were significantly correlated with job satisfaction (all resulting in positive correlations, meaning that higher support was associated with higher job satisfaction): the clarity of mission (0.28); religious beliefs and strength from God (0.21); satisfaction from seeing results of work (0.19); freedom to do things considered important (0.19); providing an important service for the community (0.16); the intellectual challenge of the ministry (0.14); and support from other local homosexual clergy (0.13).

Specific support items and type of stipend

Table 4.12 presents the data for each support item according to the type of stipend. The 0 or 'not relevant' responses were included in the calculation of these scores.

Table 4.12 Support factors according to type of stipend

Support item	Incumbent	Team vicar/ priest-in-charge	Curate	Other types
Freedom/autonomy	3.8	4.2	4.1	4.1
Non-religious friends	3.7	3.9	4.0	4.5
Religious beliefs	4.0	4.1	4.1	4.0
Seeing the results of work	3.8	4.2	4.1	4.2
Local homosexual clergy	3.4	3.1	3.2	2.9
Spouse/family	1.7	1.9	2.2	2.1
Parishioners	4.0	3.7	3.7	2.1
Clergy support groups	3.1	3.5	3.1	2.8
Intellectual challenge	3.3	3.3	3.3	3.9
Community service	3.3	3.6	3.5	3.7
Caring profession	3.1	3.3	2.5	3.4
Local heterosexual clergy	3.2	3.2	2.9	3.2
Bishop	3.2	2.7	2.1	2.5
Thoroughness of training	3.1	2.6	3.1	2.8
Clarity of mission	3.0	3.3	2.8	3.5
Total support score	49.7	50.6	48.6	49.7

Specific support items and location of parish

Table 4.13 provides a picture of the support factors of clergy in each of the parish types or locations.

Table 4.13 Support factors for clergy in different parish locations

Support item	Rural	Suburban	London/ Southwark	Other urban
Freedom/autonomy	3.8	4.2	3.7	4.1
Non-religious friends	4.1	3.9	3.9	4.0
Religious beliefs	4.1	4.1	3.9	4.1
Seeing the results of work	3.9	4.1	3.8	4.0
Local homosexual clergy	2.8	2.7	3.8	3.2
Spouse/family	1.5	1.7	2.4	1.6
Parishioners	4.0	3.8	3.3	3.7
Clergy support groups	3.3	2.3	3.1	3.3
Intellectual challenge	3.2	3.6	3.3	3.6
Community service	3.3	3.6	3.5	3.4
Caring profession	3.6	3.2	3.0	3.1
Local heterosexual clergy	3.1	3.0	3.2	3.3
Bishop	3.0	2.9	2.7	2.8
Thoroughness of training	3.1	3.4	2.9	2.8
Clarity of mission	3.0	3.0	2.9	3.4
Total support score	49.5	49.4	49.6	50.4

Sexual drive and channels for release

There were two questions relating to sexual drive. One asked the clergy to rate how highly sexed they felt they were on a 5-point scale (5 = very highly sexed; 1 = not at all sexed). The other asked them to rate the extent to which they were able to release sexual tension (5 = very frustrated/few channels for release; 1 = very sufficient channels for release).

The mean 'sexual drive' score obtained was 3.8 (with scores ranging from 2 to 5): 4 per cent scored 2; 28 per cent scored 3; 58 per cent scored 4; and 10 per cent scored 5.

The mean 'sexual release or frustration' score was 2.8: 14 per cent scored 1 indicating sufficient channels for release; 29 per cent scored 2; 23 per cent scored 3; 26 per cent scored 4; and 8 per cent scored 5, indicating a high level of frustration.

There was no statistical relationship at all between sexual drive and sexual frustration,[24] suggesting that the level of drive is not related to the perceived channels for release of drive. Neither sexual drive nor frustration scores were significantly associated with total work-demand scores, total work-support scores or total sexuality demands. The degree of sexual frustration was, however, predictive of job satisfaction,[25] showing that higher sexual frustration was associated with lower job satisfaction. The frustration score was also correlated with each of the strain scale scores.[26] In each case higher frustration was associated with higher strain scores. The level of sexual drive showed no relationships with these strain scores.

The frustration score was statistically significantly lower for those individuals who lived with a same-sex partner (mean score = 2.1) compared to those who did not (mean score = 3.1). None of the clergy living with a same-sex partner scored the maximum frustration score of 5, and only 15 per cent scored 4. In contrast, 11 per cent of those who did not live with the same-sex partner produced the maximum score, with a further 30 per cent scoring 4. Reported sexual drive scores were not affected by this domestic factor (mean score live with = 3.9; not live with = 3.7).

Mean frustration scores were generally lower for curates (mean score = 2.4) compared to other job types (incumbents = 3; team vicar/priest-in-charge = 2.9; others 2.8), although there were no such differences in the pattern of sexual drive scores. There were also significant differences in frustration scores with type of parish: clergy in the dioceses of London and Southwark had the mean lowest score of 2.4, compared to 3.2 for those in rural parishes, 3.1 for other urban and 3 for suburban locations. Only 3 per cent of those in London/Southwark scored the maximum 5, compared to 14 per cent of those in rural parishes. There were no apparent differences in sexual-drive scores for different types of parish.

The causes of psychopathology in homosexual clergy

It is not possible to assert unambigously which, if any, of the stressors investigated in this study cause the high levels of psychopathology observed: the correlational evidence is suggestive, but not conclusive. There are some powerful statistical techniques, however, which can be utilised to make the picture a little clearer, although with these, too, the interpretation is all important. One such tool used here is stepwise multiple regression. This helps to show which stressors contribute most in predicting each of the strains. It suggests which factors are most significant and at the same time employs methods which exclude those which do not make their own independent contribution. The technique was used with each of the strain measures of general anxiety, depression, somaticism and job satisfaction. For each of these strain measures the role of a whole array of possible factors was investigated simultaneously: each of the 15 work demands, 11 sexuality demands, the 15 support factors, age, weight, height, sexual frustration score, and sexual drive. If any of these factors do predict the strain levels, the stepwise regression will show this as well as suggesting their order of importance.

Job satisfaction

Of all the 46 factors considered, 8 showed up in the analysis as being particularly predictive of job satisfaction. In order of importance these were 'Being unsure about my role makes my job demanding' (despite the fact that clergy did not rate this item highly as a demand), sexual frustration, parishioners' lack of interest, funerals, marriages, etc., unsure faith, seeing results of work, support from family/spouse and isolation.

General anxiety

Of the 46 factors, 8 were revealed by the stepwise technique. In order of importance these were: being unclear about role, sexual frustration, 'public face', conceal sexuality from bishop, individual parishioners, support from parishioners and local heterosexual clergy, and community hostility.

Depression

Seven factors were independently contributing to the prediction of depression scores: putting on a 'public face', sexual frustration, support from religious beliefs, unclear work role, concealing sexuality from bishop and from family/wife/children, and the sheer load of work.

Somaticism

The best predictors were the lack of a clear division between work and home life, the demands of individual parishioners, concealing homosexuality from other priests, putting on a 'public face', concealing sexuality from family/wife/children, clergy support groups and being unclear about work role.

Discussion of the findings

This study is probably unique, in so far as it is the first systematic attempt to evaluate the size of the stress problem among Church of England homosexual clergy, and to attempt to determine some possible causes. It has been a salutary exercise, and the findings are not good news. It is hoped that the Church of England can find some value in the research and evaluate it in a positive spirit. There are undoubtedly people in responsible positions in the Church who will cast doubt on the validity of the findings, and others who will see them as a vindication for increasing the pressure to eliminate homosexual clergy from the Church. This is all too clear from my own readings of the various General Synod debates which formed part of my researches when writing this book. This research project was done to evaluate whether or not homosexual clergy were under stress (for my own part I have to admit that I doubted this at the outset of the pilot study). It has become clear since the survey was completed that the issues raised have great emotional significance for all parties concerned in the Church, and that there are many entrenched attitudes. Reading Synod proceedings on the issue was a depressing experience. The position that there can be no such thing as a practising homosexual priest was something I was naively unaware of before the study. That the issues were so contentious was unexpected. Indeed, had I been more aware of such matters, there are some areas I would have explored further in a more systematic fashion (for example, questions about actual sexual practice). I make no apologies for this: the independence it has afforded is a strength. All benefits have costs.

There are a number of central points which can be drawn from the data reported here. It should be clear that homosexual clergy form a significant minority of Church of England clergy: the 390 questionnaires themselves represent nearly 4 per cent of stipendiary clergy, and this was only a small sample of the homosexual clergy population. It is certainly ridiculous to assert, as some have, that only about 20 Church of England clergy are homosexually active.[27]

One can question the representativeness of the sample of clergy used as the basis for this report. It appears that the homosexual clergy are somewhat younger than the average profile one would expect from a random sample such as that obtained in the study of parochial clergy. This, however, could be due to the reluctance of older clergy to admit to an outside party that they are homosexual. It could also be due to an over-representation of clergy from London and Southwark (whither younger homosexual clergy may gravitate). Whatever the correct interpretation, it should be borne in mind that we are not talking about particularly young clergy: the average age of the respondents was over 45 years, with 35 per cent being over 50. These are not immature people who lack experience of life: the ACCM guidelines for the selection of candidates for the ministry highlight the need for maturity and the many benefits of balanced outlook this brings.[28]

The other relevant aspect of representativeness is whether or not the levels of strain reported here reflect the position of homosexual clergy in general. The comparison of the results of the pilot study and the principal study suggest, if anything, that the strain levels among the homosexual clergy are somewhat higher than that reported in the principal study. The pilot study was performed on a 'captive audience', while the principal study relied on people completing and sending back the questionnaires. If there is such response-bias operating, it would strongly support the view that homosexual clergy as a whole are more stressed than reported in the principal study. It is equally possible, however, that those attending the support groups (as in the pilot study) are more stressed and attend them as a form of self-therapy or coping behaviour. Since the purpose of the groups is religious, and not explicitly therapeutic, it is difficult to estimate this aspect. The claim that this sample does not represent the views of most homosexual clergy implies that there are in fact quite large numbers of homosexual clergy.

It should also not be forgotten that there are many women clergy in the Church of England (about 1,000 women deacons, for example). The study reported above was based almost entirely on a male sample. It is likely that lesbians, too, will have problems, but since only one completed the questionnaire little can be said about their experience.

Whatever the view of homosexual clergy adopted by the Church of England, it seems clear from this study that the strain (stress) levels among them are extremely high. The levels of anxiety, depression and physical manifestations of stress are a major cause for concern. While it appeared from the study of parochial clergy reported in Chapter 2 that clergy in general have quite low levels of strain, the homosexual clergy show disturbingly high levels: as many as 34 per cent of clergy in some parish locations were significantly depressed; 21 per cent of suburban clergy were suffering from general anxiety conditions; one in three curates were likely to have anxiety conditions and one in four were depressed; more than one in three of the clergy in rural locations had felt as though they were going to have a nervous breakdown, in the preceding year, with as many as 44 per cent of priests-in-charge/team vicars and 32 per cent of curates having the same feeling. The position of incumbents was significantly better, but even among these one in five had recently felt as though they were going to have a nervous breakdown, and about the same proportion suffered from depression or general anxiety. Definite intervention and practical support would seem warranted. One would expect no less from any caring employer.

The majority of the clergy in the sample were single (89 per cent), although 87 per cent of parochial clergy in the study in Chapter 2 were married. Only 25 per cent of the homosexual clergy reported living with a same-sex partner (although a number reported keeping two homes, or living with their partner on non-working days), and there was some indication from the data that those who did so benefited psychologically in terms of mental health. Those who lived with their partner also showed lower levels of sexual frustration, they were less affected by felt isolation and they did not perceive parishioners' traditionalism as so much of a demand as those who did not live with a same-sex partner. It should be noted that sexual frustration was a major predictor of job satisfaction, general anxiety and depression. This sexual frustration may promote or encourage deviant sexual behaviours (such as seeking sexual contacts in public lavatories) if the clergy feel they cannot have a permanent relationship, due to fear of others finding out. It is also likely that the Church views on homosexuality are actually partly responsible for such behaviours, since they equate long-term relationships with promiscuity (see the discussion in Chapter 6 on the Higton debate). Long-term relationships are much more visible than 'one night stands', and the homosexual priest concerned about being exposed may be prompted into behaviours he also finds uncongenial, but unavoidable.

The average Body Mass Index (weight in kilos/height in metres squared) of the clergy was 24.6, which is within an acceptable weight range. The clergy were also relatively abstemious as far as alcohol and cigarette consumption were concerned. It would appear that obesity or such substance abuse was unlikely to contribute to the high strain levels observed; in fact, given the stress levels, these figures might well have been expected to be much higher.

Despite the high strain levels, the clergy were surprisingly satisfied with their jobs: only 14 per cent scored below the mid-point on the scale. This should not be taken as evidence that the stress problem is not a major one since it is known that job satisfaction and strain are not necessarily related.[29] Both rural clergy and curates appeared less satisfied than the average (these groups also evidenced more psychological strain in terms of anxiety, depression, somaticism and nervous breakdown feelings which suggests they should be the particular focus of concern).

The relatively poor situation for rural clergy probably reflects the effects of their isolation from individuals of like sexuality. They scored more highly on the 'isolation' work demand item than clergy from other locations, and also reported high levels of demand from having to put on a 'public face'. The demands of running a rural parish require the clergy to be an integral part of the social network of the parish and their sexuality would place particular demands upon them in this respect. The fact that rural clergy also found funerals, marriages, etc. more demanding than clergy in other locations probably reflects their social centrality in the community they serve.

It is important to recognise that social isolation is likely to have effects on all clergy, irrespective of the location of their parish. Although the 'isolation' demand was only ranked 7th in terms of work demands, 15 per cent of the clergy gave it a 5-rating. Twenty per cent also gave a 5-rating to the demands of continually having to put on a 'public face'. The lack of adequate social relationships has been shown to affect the ability of the immune system to fight infections and cancer.[30] Loneliness has been identified as a particular stressor in married American pastors (and their wives),[31] and one can only suppose the condition to be worse for homosexual clergy in the Church of England. Many of the clergy were extrovert personality types (as suggested by the high levels of 'hysteria' in the pilot sample) which would probably compound the negative effects of isolation: individuals with an over-dependence on others without the social context of support required. There is certainly a wealth of evidence showing the importance of social support in health and well-being,[32] and research on homosexual men suggests that they may be immune-deficient as a result of stress resulting from a lack of community support, an inability to express feelings, and a negative self-image.[33]

The work demand which was ranked highest was that the job required more time than there was available to do it in (36 per cent gave this a 5-rating). The sheer load of work was ranked second. Clearly the clergy perceive their work-load as rather high, which may help dispel the popular view that clergy only work on Sundays! Individual parishioners seem to add significantly to the work demands. 'Being unsure about faith' came bottom of the demands list, and, although two or three individuals were obviously going through a crisis of faith, the clergy were extremely sure about their religious convictions. A number of the work demands were correlated with the strain scales (anxiety, depression, somaticism, nervous breakdown feeling, job satisfaction). It would seem likely that work demands were contributing factors to strain levels, even though the statistical associations were in the main rather modest. It also appears (and should come as no surprise) that the demands perceived as being most significant were not necessarily the ones which predicted strain levels. The demands which best predicted strain levels were role ambiguity, having to put on a 'public face', and individual parishioners.

The work demands placed upon the clergy due to their sexuality were perceived as being very significant, and higher total sexuality demands were associated with higher levels of general anxiety, depression and somaticism. The clergy saw the established Church views on sexuality as having a major impact on their job demand (given a 5-rating by 42 per cent), although this item did not seem to be related to the strain scores. While this suggests that it did not play a significant role in the mental health of the clergy,[34] the high profile clergy gave the factor makes it a cause for concern. Considerable concern was also expressed about the media finding out about their sexuality, although this factor too did not seem to play a role in well-being. The level of perceived community hostility to homosexuals was also perceived as demanding, as well as being predictive of general anxiety. Interestingly, not being open with the bishop about their sexuality was not rated very highly as a demand (ranked eleventh) but was a predictor of depression and general anxiety.

There were a number of differences between the level of sexuality demands for different stipendiary types and parish locations. Community hostility was perceived as being a significantly lower demand for clergy in London and Southwark, as were the effects of having to espouse views in public which were at odds with their own sexuality. Urban clergy (including London) did not suffer as much from having to conceal their sexuality from their parishioners, or from the traditionalism of their parishioners. This is probably due to the fact that the urban areas are more liberal and cosmopolitan, with the consequent effect that homosexual clergy are not as 'visible'. In general, the incumbents and curates had much higher scores on most sexuality demands.

Total perceived support was correlated with depression scores such that higher levels of job support were associated with lower depression. The specific support factors related to high strain levels were supports from seeing the results of their work, religious beliefs and strength from

God, knowing they are providing an important service to the community, knowing they are part of a caring profession, and the clarity of their mission. Of these, the support derived from their religious beliefs appeared to be the most important predictor of strain. This factor was give a 5-rating by 37 per cent of the clergy and was ranked fifth overall. Interpersonal support factors also figure as important for clergy, with (perhaps surprisingly) support from non-religious friends high on the list of supports. Autonomy and freedom were also considered important to the clergy, although this, too, did not show any associations with strain, but did correlate with job satisfaction. Previous research[35] demonstrates that lack of autonomy or job discretion is an important predictor of coronary heart disease and its precursors, especially when considered in conjunction with the level of job demand, and the high levels of autonomy shown by the clergy could be construed as an important buffer for the high levels of perceived workload and time constraints.

There were some significant effects of type of work and parish location on perceived job support. Incumbents reported lower levels of support from non-religious friends than others, but higher support from their parishioners. Curates reported particularly low levels of support from their bishop, from the clarity of their mission, and from knowing they are part of a caring profession. Interestingly, the support obtained from the intellectual challenge of the mission was highest for the 'other stipendiary' types, which is probably a consequence of the greater variety in their jobs, which included chaplains, monks, Synod staff and cathedral clergy. Clergy in urban locations, including London/Southwark, reported higher support from local homosexual clergy, presumably because they are usually geographically closer. Clergy in the dioceses of London and Southwark reported less support from parishioners than those in other locations, which may reflect the fact that they do not become as enmeshed in the local social networks. Some of the support factors were also affected by whether or not the clergy lived with a same-sex partner. For example, the support of their religious beliefs and strength from God was lower if the clergy lived with a partner. This may be due to such clergy being able to count on the support of a significant other, with the consequence that they need less support from their religious beliefs.

Overall, the evidence reported here presents a very depressing picture of the health and well-being of homosexual clergy in the Church of England. The degree of culpability of the Church is less clear, although it seems unambiguously to have a duty to discharge as a caring employer. This duty should be considered a matter of great urgency.

Notes

1. Babuscio, 1988.
2. See p. 110.
3. See the estimates below concerning the prevalence of homosexuality among Church of England clergy.
4. Based on Fay, Turner, Klassen and Gagnon, 1989.
5. See, for example, Babuscio, 1988.
6. The Gloucester Report also says as much in paragraph 113.
7. Fletcher, 1990.
8. *Church of England Year Book*, 1988.
9. The correlation was —0.36, which is highly significant.
10. For this comparison the scores are compared to the norms provided in Crown and Crisp, 1979 for men, aged 45–54, from a general population study. Given the effects of social class (the higher the social class, the less strain – see Fletcher, 1988a), this comparison is likely to be somewhat conservative.
11. Assessed by elevated scores on the CCEI and TFQ scales.
12. CCEI norms from Crown and Crisp, 1979.
13. CCEI norms from *ibid*.
14. *Ibid*.; Stone, 1985.
15. For example, total work-demand correlated with the 'thoughts and feelings' scales, +0.39 for anxiety, +0.38 for depression, and +0.29 for somatic anxiety (all highly significant).
16. Correlation (r) = —0.25, $p <$ 0.001.
17. $r = +0.20$.
18. As measured by the TFQ.
19. Correlations = —0.26; —0.36; —0.30; —0.29; —0.14 respectively.
20. The correlations were +0.22 with anxiety ($p < 0.002$), +0.18 with depression ($p < 0.009$) and +0.16 with somaticism ($p < 0.018$).
21. $r =$ —0.18; —0.19; —0.17 respectively.
22. $r =$ —0.18.
23. $r = +0.21$.
24. $r =$ —0.04.
25. $r =$ —0.19.
26. For example, the frustration score was correlated with free-floating anxiety = +0.26; with depression = +0.29; with somatic anxiety = +0.16, on the CCEI scales.
27. Reverend David Holloway, General Synod, 11 November, 1987, Proceedings, p. 935.
28. ACCM, Occasional Paper, No. 12, June 1983.
29. Kasl, 1978.
30. Kennedy, Kiecolt-Glaser and Glaser, 1988.
31. Warner and Carter, 1984.
32. Payne and Jones, 1987.
33. Cecchi, 1984.
34. Although the lack of association may be a result of ceiling effects.
35. Fletcher, 1988a; Karasek, 1979.

5

A Case Study and Quotations

This chapter attempts to bring some of the findings of the study of stress among homosexual clergy into the personal domain. So far many different tables and figures have been presented to demonstrate that the clergy are under great strain, and why this might be so. What, however, do they feel like in their situation? What are the human and spiritual costs for them? Are they concerned about their situation? How has being homosexual affected their work and their views of the Church? This chapter addresses these and other issues in two ways. First, it presents a selection of the spontaneous written comments made by the clergy at the end of their questionnaire. Second, one clergyman has kindly written down some of his own feelings and experiences about being a homosexual priest. I am greatly indebted to him for letting us share these thoughts: I am sure they were not written without some emotional cost.

Written comments made by clergy

At the end of the questionnaire, clergy were invited to add comments if they wished, although it was not in any sense required that they should do so. This invitation is often extended as a courtesy by the questionnaire designer without any expectation that anything will be written or the content analysed. In this case, however, so many depressing and negative comments were appended, that it was felt necessary to present a selection of them to provide the reader with a sense of some of the difficulties and feelings the individuals were experiencing. In reproducing these comments I have not selectively edited out any positive ones:

the comments are selected, but not selective. I have not included any comments which related to sexual activity or expressed sexual predilections, although a number were made implying that the Church's views on sexuality were causing some clergy sexual difficulties.

I was taken aback at the depth of feeling and the expressions of dissatisfaction with the way the Church of England is portrayed as dealing with homosexual clergy. A surprising number of the priests also said they had had breakdowns, not just felt as though they might. In a number of these cases the Church (or bishop) was praised for the help that had been given. It is not my intention to discuss the comments at all: the readers can draw their own conclusions from what was written. I begin on a positive note.

'Yes, life is difficult because of one's sexuality. *But* being a priest is a great privilege with tremendous job satisfaction – and I wouldn't change from this vocation!'

'I am very glad to say it is the Church that has the problems!'

'I am now in my early fifties and feel the best years are past and the state of the Church and society give little encouragement for the future.'

'From my replies it will not be a surprise to learn that I have been engaged in psychotherapy for some time. The stress and neurosis is a blessing in some ways because it is the motive for change.'

'It is really difficult – despite one's vocation – remaining *within* the Church. Guilt sometimes has a field-day, but how much of that is what the Church would really like to do to me to make it feel better?'

'Fear of betrayal ranks high in the anxiety stakes and I find it difficult to trust others, especially heterosexual men (usually priest-colleagues). You will see from my questionnaire that I regard bishops as about the most useless creatures in the universe. You can never believe what you are told about "confidentiality" – the closet, despite its appalling pressures, is a good deal better than your Diocese treating you as a leper, a potential scandal, or an unexploded bomb.'

'Thank you for caring enough to do this survey: it will undoubtedly uncover crushing pastoral needs, unmet by the Church.'

'My therapist has been my greatest asset for the last eight months!'

'After the November 1987 General Synod vote I felt like resigning from the parish. I haven't as yet, but I would seriously like to leave, if my responsibilities to the churchwardens and the parish were completed.'

'The "Higton" debate makes applying for jobs difficult. You *know* bishops are shying away from *ALL* single clergy except in tough posts where we are good enough!'

'My view of the Church of England is at an all-time *low*.'

'Most of my anxiety is concerned with the media discovering I am a homosexual priest, and what that could mean. This makes me afraid to enter into a stable homosexual relationship...'

'The worst feeling is that of loneliness. I long for a one-to-one friendship but this could not be whilst I am an incumbent... I long to meet someone of the same sex with whom I can share my life... I am planning an early retirement... perhaps then I can look forward to a little happiness and peace.'

'As a solitary priest, without [personal therapy]... I'd have "gone under" long ago.'

'Basically, apart from a handful of friends who love you enough to accept you as you are, you are *on your own*, serving a repressive institution which lacks moral courage and won't take risks... I feel I'm still undergoing a long process of emotional crucifixion: but if you're basically honest and sincere it's a slap in the face to your integrity to have to live a lie. *God* knows the score – I'm honest with him...'

'Thanks for taking the trouble to find out what we are up against.'

'My nervous breakdown was caused by stress – my sexuality being contributory amongst other factors.'

'I am concerned about the lack of understanding within the Church about sexuality in all its aspects. There seems to be so much denial of anxiety and fear about the sexuality of so many individuals within the Church. The difficulty seems to be that the denial is, in most cases, not acknowledged; and the sad thing is that Scripture is so often used as a defence against the denial. Could it be that this is the root cause of so much stress in the Church?'

'Much of the stress I experience at work has little to do with being gay – except when the subject becomes the major debate of the Synod and some of its fundamentalist clergy – but from the sheer pressure of the workload. That's not to say that living a dual existence does not have its problems.'

'There are some things I am totally certain about; despite the Church, God has chosen me as his priest; I am loved and accepted as I am.'

'I often feel a "dinosaur" living in a hostile and rejecting environment. Is it worth the hassle? "Mustn't hurt (hit) Mother (Church)." "Mother Church" switches from "nurturing" to "critical" and "devouring". Why should I... be made a scapegoat to make the Church feel better? I am increasingly concerned by the lie of the purity of the official Church – it is a hypocritical stance...'

'I used to be a victim of depression, but since I found a partner who really cares I've not been troubled for years... (stress) is much more to do with the way the Church is going... than anything to do with sexual orientations or frustrations.'

'What I find distressing is the lack of openness in the Church and the impersonal nature of many contacts.'

'The main source of stress for me – I think – is that I have too much work to do and too much of it is problems personal to people or administration.'

'I shall finish off the work begun... My bishop, archdeacon, and area dean offer no support nor interest in the work of the parish. I feel particularly disillusioned with my bishop...'

'I have tried to live in fidelity and love (with male friend of many years standing) but the cost of doing so is not acknowledged and supported by the Church...'

'The Church's attitude to homosexuality has cost me dear. If only it would have the goodness to see that a longstanding sexual and emotional relationship with another man is as God-given as that between a man and woman. Instead it treats us like lepers who lack any emotions and equates homosexuality with promiscuity.'

The case study

The case study which follows was written by one of the priests who had completed the questionnaire. He had completed it before being asked if he would provide the thoughts below. There was no special reason for asking him other than that he was willing to do it and was known by one of my contacts. I do not wish to say much about the priest because he needs to remain anonymous for obvious reasons. With his permission, however, I was able to identify his completed questionnaire and would like to say one or two things as background. He is a middle-aged parish priest whose questionnaire answers showed him to feel under less work demand than average for the homosexual clergy, although he finds that the job requires more work than there is time to do it in, and finds the sheer load of work demanding as well as the pressures continually to create new ideas and solve problems. He gave 5-ratings to the following sexuality demands: the 'established Church views' on sexuality; worrying about the media finding out about his homosexuality; and finding promotions within the Church more unlikely because of his sexuality. He reported quite high levels of support on most fronts, but support was particularly high from other local homosexual clergy, job autonomy, strength from religious beliefs and God, support from the bishop, and from knowing he is part of a caring profession.

He does not smoke or drink alcohol regularly, is average weight for his height and had not felt as though he was going to have a nervous breakdown. His scores on the depression, anxiety and somaticism scales were low. He is not, therefore, one of the clergy with stress problems and his perceptions are not likely to be coloured by strain.

I have not cut anything from his accounts, and the title is his. I am very grateful for what has been provided. Such accounts take courage, incur painful emotions, and take time. Thank you.

Practice makes perfect – confessions of a homosexual priest

'I am a priest of the Church of England and, for some reason best known to the Lord, I am also homosexual. That poses a dilemma for the Church in general and for the Church of England in particular. Those in authority would prefer to ignore my existence – and the existence of a significant number of clergy like myself – to say nothing of the even greater number of men and women who are homosexual and try to live a Christian life.

The Church can just about accept us if we are celibate; she can cope with us if we confess the occasional misdemeanour and seek forgiveness; but if we are living together in faithful, permanent, committed partnerships then there are those who would have us hounded out of the Body of Christ. I know that a witch-hunt exists because I have been a victim of it. This chapter is written in the hope that the facts of my life may lead others to see that to be Christian and homosexual are not incompatible, nor is celibacy compulsory for all of us.

Archbishop William Temple declared that Christianity is the most materialistic of the world's religions; a gloss on the words of St John's Gospel: 'The Word was made flesh and dwelt among us.' It is therefore ironic that this same Christianity has found the flesh so difficult to handle. For much of its history, the Church has heeded certain words of St Paul and St Augustine, rather than treading in the steps of Jesus Christ. Someone has remarked that if only St Augustine had made an honest woman of his mistress, then the Church's attitude to sex might have been very different. Instead, there has been a fear of human sexuality in general, and of homosexuality in particular. Yet the Jewish–Christian tradition is truest both to itself and to the Lord when it emphasises the unity of body and soul. In a real sense, we do not just have a body – each one of us is our body: all we are and all we seek to express must be conveyed by means of our flesh and blood. Our sexual orientation is therefore an inevitable and significant part of our life and our approach to daily living.

In 1989, ten years after the publication of the Gloucester Report, *Homosexual Relationships*, the Church of England finds it hard officially to accept that anyone can be a practising Christian and at the same time homosexual; to be one of that Church's priests and homosexual is the ultimate sin against the Holy Spirit. I write this knowing that the Lord (through his Holy Spirit) has led me to be a priest, and that the exercise of His priesthood has been enhanced, not hindered, by the fact that I am homosexual and have been committed to my partner in a faithful, permanent relationship for over twenty years. The rest of this chapter will spell out in detail how I can reconcile my lifestyle with my own conscience, as well as with the teaching of the Bible and the tradition of the Church; both of which are usually cited in order to condemn any such homosexual relationship as being against God's holy law.

Each of us treads the road of life in this world only once, and we have to make some sense of the way things are for us. We do not walk alone, because there is the common experience of human history for us to learn from; and Christians also have the tradition of the Church as well as the Scriptures to guide them. Yet, if each of us is a unique individual, precious in God's sight, then how do I come to terms with life – realising that I am not as most men are? Instead, I am one of a minority, albeit a significant one, which has been persecuted in most generations by both Church and State.

Some people have tried to prove that either nature or nurture, or both, make certain men and women homosexual. As far as I am concerned, God alone knows why I am one of those who can relate only to someone of their own sex where any meaningful partnership is involved. I have grown up this way, and can point to no incident which has 'made' me homosexual. No one has ever abused me or interfered with me; indeed, I can recall no time when I was not attracted to those of my own sex, but my formative years were a time when my eyes were set on celibacy in the Catholic tradition. Not that I was segregated from the female sex: all my schooling and student days from the age of 5 till 23 were spent in co-education. About the age of 19 or 20, the truth began to dawn on me when I read a description of what it means to be homosexual: 'Briefly, it is that I am attracted towards men, in the way in which most men are attracted towards women' (Peter Wildeblood, *Against the Law*, Penguin Books, 1959 (reprint), p. 8). I knew at once that this described my own deepest feelings. Several times I had dated women in the hope that something might click. Now I began to realise that that side of life was closed to me. Still, in those days before the reform of 1967, I kept myself to myself, and never frequented any gay pubs or clubs. I saw myself as a confirmed bachelor, who would be dedicated to whatever work I undertook.

During my years as a teacher, my vocation to the priesthood returned. This was a relief, because here was a way of life which catered for the single state; I could be a priest or a religious, and not have to explain why I was not married and unlikely ever to be so. This ideal survived my years at theological college, but not my first year in a parish. Not for the first time, I fell in love with another man; but, for the very first time, it was mutual. Hitherto, I had only had crushes on those who were in no position to reciprocate my feelings. In my late twenties, I found myself beginning a relationship which has been as close to marriage as is possible for two men devoted to each other. As with any relationship, there have been moments of difficulty and tension, but the partnership has flourished for over twenty years, and we are both convinced that God has done more with us together than He could have done with either of us separately.

How can I live such a lifestyle, and still believe in the Bible? Mainly because the Bible does not condemn homosexuality as a way of life for a significant minority of men and women. All the references in the Old and New Testaments can be understood as referring to homosexual behaviour which involves temple prostitution as practised by the pagans, and thus abhorrent to the Jews; or as the indulging in such behaviour by people who were normally heterosexual. Jesus himself never mentions the subject. He did, however, promise that His Holy Spirit would be with us always to lead us into the complete truth. If homosexual orientation as we know it was unknown to the writers and editors of the Scriptures then it is quite possible to argue that a permanent, faithful, committed relationship between two men or women is compatible with the teaching of the Bible, God and His Truth are not trapped within the covers of the Bible, and if the Holy Spirit guides you to read not just the words of Scripture, but also to read between the lines, then it is reasonable to see homosexual partnerships as part of God's purpose for some people.

Of course, there are fundamentalists in the Church of England and elsewhere who refuse to enter into any kind of dialogue or debate, because for them the words of Scripture leave no room for doubt. What E. Lear said about the Church of Scotland is as true of at least part of the Church of England: 'The Word made Flesh is thus made word again.' The Church of England, however, has never officially based its doctrine on the Bible alone. I, too, believe in the Bible; but I believe also in God's continuing revelation through His Church. If His Holy Spirit is still leading us into all truth, then there is room for interpretation and development; were this not so, the Church would even now be teaching that slavery is a viable option for some human beings.

How do I reconcile my lifestyle with the tradition of the Church? Once again I appeal to the work of the Holy Spirit, leading us into a fuller understanding of God's truth revealed in Jesus Christ. Tradition is not only something that is handed on, but also something that has to be received by each generation and interpreted in ways which each generation can understand. Tradition can therefore develop, and our modern understanding of homosexual orientation need not be against the Church's tradition. Some words of Dr J. Dominian in his recent book *Sexual Integrity* are relevant here:

there is always the nightmare for the Christian that, however clear the teaching on homosexuality appears to be, it might be open to essential modification, in which case we are placing false burdens on these men and women. The thought is haunting. So that in the matter of homosexuality, as in many other sexual issues, we have to watch and pray. On the one hand we must not lightly dismiss traditional teaching and on the other we must be conscious that in all matters – but particularly sexual ones – the need to see morality in a new light is a constant and urgent matter. It is imperative for the Church to teach with authority; it is equally imperative to examine this teaching responsibility in the light of the ever-evolving understanding of human nature and scriptural hermeneutics. (p. 28)

When the Gloucester Report was published in 1979, I had great hopes that this would lead to reasoned debate at all levels in the Church, from parish discussion groups and Parish Church Councils right up to General Synod. A decade later, we now know that the report was shelved; the issue was not faced. Nor did General Synod face it in November 1987 when the Revd. Tony Higton's motion sparked off a debate which has since led to the very kind of witch-hunt he denied he was seeking. If Higton rules, then it is not OK for the Church of England. If the Church in general and the ordained ministry in particular are to be purged as he wishes, then the Church of England will be reduced to an exclusive Puritan sect, consisting only of the self-righteous who are assured that they alone are saved.

'There is no fear in love, but perfect love casts out fear' (I John 4.18). The present climate in the Church of England is casting out that perfect love which is possible for homosexual partnerships as for heterosexual marriages. There is a climate of deception and dishonesty among Bishops and their clergy as all attempt to present a respectable face to the world. This is hardly the way Christ's Family should behave. Were all homosexual clergy to be forced to resign, then the Church of England would lose many of its priests. There would be less 'faith in the city' because such priests tend to work in those parts of the Church which married clergy prefer not to reach.

The problem, however, goes far beyond the clergy. If there are many homosexual clergy, then there are many more homosexual lay men and women. The Church's attitude is making their already difficult lifestyle even more painful. Were the Church brave enough to offer an ethic for homosexuals which emphasises the fulfilment to be found in permanent, faithful, committed relationships, then this would indeed by a heaven-sent relief for many of God's sons and daughters. People like myself are caught in a situation from which we cannot escape. We have to keep our heads down, and try to minister in Christ's name as if we were the ordinary, heterosexual beings that both Church and society would like us to be.

It has been very hurtful for me to be told by certain bishops that I am not wanted because I am homosexual; my sexual orientation apparently invalidates all that I am as a priest. Until a recent crisis, I had for most of my twenty years in parish work enjoyed great job satisfaction. I now believe some parts of the Church and its hierarchy are no longer expressing the mind of Christ. The Church of England has always prided itself on being an open Church in which there is room for discussion and difference of opinion. Homosexuality seems to be one topic on which there is no room for divergence of views. The past decade has seen divorced clergy remarried and serving in those very dioceses where the bishop is against gay clergy; these bishops would point to Scripture in order to support their stand, yet in the gospels our Lord says nothing about homosexuality but a great deal about divorce and adultery.

I was recently prevented from moving to a new parish, even though I had been offered the job and accepted it, and the whole thing had become public knowledge. The bishop had been informed by one of my relations that I was living in a homosexual partnership of over twenty years' duration. The said bishop had declared publicly at the time of his appointment that he would never knowingly ordain or license anyone who was a practising homosexual. I pointed out that this was a blanket term which in the popular mind implied promiscuity, and that my situation was very different. While admitting that it was unfortunate that the facts had come to his attention via a private informer and not through any public scandal, he nevertheless refused to go back on his original decision and opinion. In the Church of England today, a priest is only as safe as his diocesan bishop allows him to be. Some bishops are very understanding and supportive; and are prepared to dismiss as soon as they learn of your sexual orientation and practice.

This puts a lot of pressure on all gay clergy, and especially on those who are in permanent, faithful relationships. We are sitting targets for certain Sunday newspapers unless we are totally secretive about our private life. I would claim that by the grace of God I am as good a priest as He can make me *because* I am homosexual, and not in spite of it. My faithful commitment to a partner allows me to sympathise more readily with the bereaved at funerals, because I can imagine how I would feel if my partner had died. I can rejoice in those seeking to be married, because I know what a joy it is to be committed wholly to another human being. There are moments, of course, when all is not sweetness and light, but even those occasions can be faced and lived through; and the relationship can emerge wiser and stronger from the experience. This is not to deny that there is a place for celibacy, but that is a vocation to which some are called, and can never be a condition that is imposed upon anyone. I simply make the point that because I am homosexual and have a partner God can work through the two of us in a more fruitful way than if we had not been so committed to Him and to each other.

I consider myself fortunate that my life has turned out the way it has.

There are too many gay clergy (and laity) who have got married in the hope that this would somehow be a 'cure'. All too often these are the ones who fall foul of the law in public lavatories. Gay priests who are unwilling or unable to live in a permanent relationship must suffer, unless they can positively commit themselves to celibacy and perhaps find a support group, such as becoming oblates of a religious community. While those who are married or are celibate have enjoyed a recognised status in the Church, those of us who are homosexual have to fend for ourselves. Support groups do exist, but these have to be unofficial and secret. Can those in authority in the Church not see that the failure to provide any ethic for gay Christians leaves them with no meaningful guidelines; and thus in a situation in which it is easy to let recklessness have full rein? If there is nothing to aim at or hope for, then desperate actions too often follow.

Churchmanship in the Church of England also has tragic effects upon both extremes, Catholic and Evangelical. Until recently when a support group was formed, Evangelical gay clergy were far worse off than their Catholic counterparts because Protestantism has rarely had any place for the single state, and never any acceptance of homosexuality. On the Catholic wing there can also be intolerance. Traditional moral theology has been able to cope with those who confess their sins; thus it has been permissible to live a life that is a series of one-night stands and fleeting relationships, each of which is repented of and confessed; whereas those who seek to maintain permanent and faithful partnerships are totally condemned. There can also be hostility from those clergy who have married to cure or camouflage their own sexual preferences; they are very loud in condemning those who are enjoying what they would have liked to enjoy.

My greatest frustration is that I cannot share the fact of my love with those among whom I minister. Many may guess; a chosen few actually know; most would probably accept me and my partner for what we are. Unfortunately in 1989 in England, and especially in the Church of England, homosexuality still remains 'the love that dare not speak its name'. I am vulnerable in a way that touches the very heart of my being, and this can be distressing and demoralising. Until my recent job crisis, I had never considered myself to be particularly stressed or near to breakdown; but in recent months I have found things harder to cope with than ever before. I live in fear of being victimised within the very institution that ought to be able to accept me as I am for God's sake. If only I could make it known that it is possible to be Christian and gay, then many others in society could benefit, and there might be less prejudice and victimisation. The figure of the scapegoat may be very close to the person of Christ, but Christians today have enough to bear in His name without being persecuted because their sexual orientation does not have the approval of the majority in Church and State.

Living with my partner has all the benefits that sharing can give to such a relationship. I am fairly introvert while my partner is extrovert, so in that way we complement one another; for this reason I am convinced that God can do more with us together than He could do with either of us separately. The greatest disadvantage of living together is the practical one of holidays: two priests in one parish can hardly go away and leave the parish unattended for any length of time. It is not easy to get cover for Sundays. In fact, we manage to have one weekend and the eight days around it away together; the rest of our time off (apart from one day each week) is taken separately.

Most of my stress comes from being in an inner-city parish with all the problems of deprivation and anti-social behaviour that go with it. Personally, I do not feel stressed because of my relationship; we are able to support each other and share the joys as well as the sorrows of parish life. I have always tried to be true to myself and to my vocation. Integrity has been essential. I have had to reconcile my lifestyle with my theology; there was no question of leading a double life – keeping my private life quite unrelated to my life as a priest. For me that is impossible, though I do understand how and why some are driven to such a double existence: pious in the sanctuary, but promiscuous in the clubs, pubs and toilets. I have always tried to be honest with myself, even though I can rarely be honest with other people until they can be 'trusted' with my secret.

I am not sure how representative my views are. In my relationship, I have consciously tried to imitate what is required for a successful marriage. I believe that it is a fundamental and God-given characteristic of human nature that each of us is created for the ideal of a one-to-one partnership. It is therefore essential for a homosexual pairing to be as committed, permanent and faithful as any marriage aims to be. I am annoyed that the Church as a whole will not look at even this restricted view as a basis of an ethic for gay Christians. I owe a lot to the stability which such a relationship can provide; it offers the framework for happiness and fulfilment which promiscuous behaviour cannot give.

I think that most people – clergy and lay – who have known us for some time can accept us for what we are. The difficulty about being gay, and being known to be gay, is to find a happy medium between extremes. If our gayness is the first thing that people know about us, then that fact colours everything else they want to think or know about us. On the other hand, if they first learn to know and respect us for what we are as clergy and the work we are doing (by their fruits shall ye know them) and the gayness is the last thing to be discovered, then usually this is kept in its proper perspective. Perhaps this could be summed up as follows: why is the homosexual always labelled by his/her sexuality, whereas the heterosexual rarely is? As regards other people (family or friends, superiors or colleagues, general public or particular parishioners), being gay requires a facade until such time as a natural moment arises when they can be told. There is often acceptance, but to get beyond that stage is always a gamble – and one which is rarely risked.

God knows that the public life of a priest – especially if he serves in the inner city – has more than its fair share of stress, without his private life becoming media fodder and subject to prejudice and misunderstanding. I dare not stand up to be counted; not even in my own parish. The congregation might be sympathetic, but how would the rest of the population react? Yet how will the Church ever know what it is like to be a Christian, a priest, and gay, unless it asks me, and all the others like me? Our very lives are the evidence the Church needs in order to learn how we reconcile the way we are with the Way of Christ. When there is a climate of opinion that allows us to speak for ourselves without fear of victimisation, then and only then will the Church be able to formulate some kind of ethic and theology for homosexual men and women.'

6

What Can Be Done?

The picture painted of stress among Church of England clergy in general is not one which should cause concern. The situation of homosexual clergy, however, is very much a matter of seriousness which requires definite action and that must presumably include definite action on the part of the Church hierarchy. There is evidence that the reason for the poor state of health of homosexual clergy is a direct consequence of the way in which the Church has dealt with issues of sexuality although there is also evidence that this is exacerbated by the personalities of the clergy themselves.

The depressing findings from the study of homosexual clergy, together with the many written comments received from them, prompted me to research in some depth the way in which the Church of England had dealt with the issue of homosexuality in the recent past. The results of these investigations provided me with a greater understanding of the difficult position the homosexual clergy are in. The public deliberations of the Church have undoubtedly contributed to the high levels of stress experienced by homosexual clergy. It is for this reason that the first part of this chapter is devoted to providing some background detail about these deliberations. The second part of the chapter discusses some possible solutions to the serious situation the Church is faced with.

The public face of the Church and its attitude towards homosexual clergy

Some writers have suggested that the Church is closed and uncaring in its view of homosexuality. In 1988, Eric James, Director of Christian Action, Honorary Canon of St Albans and Chaplain to H.M. The Queen, in his document *Homosexuality and a Pastoral Church*,[1] makes a plea to the Church for the pastoral care of the homosexual by considering what had (or rather, had not) happened since 1979 when the Church of England published the Gloucester Report, *Homosexual Relations: a Contribution to Discussion*. This report was the culmination of the efforts of a very eminent working party set up by the Board for Social Responsibility in February 1974. The working party was reputed to represent all interested parties, including homosexual clergy, medics, lawyers, theologians, philosophers and social workers.

The Church of England Report received the unanimous backing of the entire working party but the Board of Social Responsibility felt it could not adopt the contents and appended 21 paragraphs of 'critical observations'. These cast doubt on some of the working party's interpretations of the biblical and theological evidence which had made some small steps towards a greater understanding and acceptance of the Christian morality of homosexual relationships. This was the first time there had been such a 'report on the Report' appended and this was interpreted by some as an indication of the negative attitudes of the Church establishment. The Report itself was undoubtedly unsatisfactory as far as most parties were concerned. Its discussion of the Scriptures would have outraged the Evangelicals within the Church, and its treatment of homosexuality may well have alienated the homosexual clergy too. It treated homosexuality as an illness (although it does say that 'Homosexuals, through no fault of their own, find themselves in a position of great difficulty, in which many of the guidelines normally available do not apply, and in which there is little general understanding or sympathy'[2]). The Report concentrated on the negative aspects of homosexuality (for example, is it condemned by the Bible, what are the legal implications, the effect on parishioners of homosexual clergy living together, what should the bishop do with homosexual clergy?) and contains little consideration of possible positive benefits: homosexual clergy are treated as 'a problem'. It gives the impression that it would rather jettison the homosexual vicar than help him work effectively in his sector or parish. The Report is also naive and impractical in places: for example, it suggests that an 'atmosphere of pastoral confidence between an ordinand and his bishop, or diocesan director of ordinands, would normally allow questions about sexuality to be broached freely'.[3]

The Report does suggest that the Church should be tolerant to the extent of reconsidering its traditional opposition to homosexual clergy, even though it explicitly makes it clear 'that we do not accept the claim to full homosexual equality – the claim that homosexual relationships and practices should be treated in all respects as equivalent to heterosexual ones'.[4] It also says, 'We would ask those who would wish the Church to condemn such homosexual relationships unreservedly to have regard to the Church's pastoral concern for those who cannot conform to the norm of marriage... we believe that the Church can and should speak pastorally and positively and present the values which can be found in different choices, while recognising also the restraint that needs to be exercised.'[5] This, apparently, has never happened. There was some debate in General Synod on the Gloucester Report on 27 February 1981 with the position of homosexual clergy being represented by one clergyman (the Reverend R. Lewis) who proclaimed, 'I cannot ditch the weight of Scripture and tradition... I cannot because it would suit me to do so... Remove the prejudice, yes, but do not, in order to put yourself in the right, maintain that black is white... [Homosexuality] is a disability. It is part of the fault of things. Homosexuality is a cheat. So it is no business of the Church or any other group to make equal what is not equal. We are considering a mystery, and a mystery which I from my dunghill can only simply hold before my Maker...'[6] The majority of homosexual clergy, however, may well have been afraid to declare themselves as such (or may not have been represented at Synod). In this sense they may have been prisoners of circumstance unable to add to a debate that was vitally affecting their position in the Church and forcing them more and more into isolation. At the February 1981 Synod, Canon D. A. Rhymes failed in his attempt to get the Gloucester Report commended for discussion in the Diocesan and Deanery Synods especially to consider the social implications and pastoral support and care.

The Higton Private Member's Motion on Sexual Morality

In November 1987, the leader of the Alliance for Biblical Witness to Our Nation, the Reverend Anthony Higton, called for the removal of practising homosexual clergy from the Church. According to James this debate was 'of tragic significance, not least because it took place without that widespread discussion in the Church at large which should have followed the publication of *Homosexual Relationships*... 10 years later, with little further study or discussion, there was the Synod declaring its mind – and individual bishops, priests and laity declaring theirs.'[7]

The Higton motion asked Synod to affirm '(ii) that fornication, adultery and homosexual acts are sinful in all circumstances; (iii) that Christian leaders are called to be exemplary in all spheres of morality, including sexual morality, as a condition of being appointed to or remaining in office'.[8] Higton attacked homosexual clergy, equating them, in the main, with highly promiscuous homosexuals, referring to his report *Sexuality and the Church*. He said in Synod, 'Very few homosexual men are in stable, faithful relationships with other men. The US Center for Disease Control in 1982 found that the average homosexual interviewed had had 555 different sexual partners, and the AIDS victims interviewed had had an average of 1,100 partners. Some were having approximately nine sexual encounters per evening... It is clear what we are dealing with in the Church is a reflection of that scene...'[9] The speech associated, by implication, the majority of homosexual clergy with the immoral and utterly promiscuous. One speaker, Mr Frank Williams, saw that the Church itself was probably responsible for some immorality because of its public attitude of condemnation towards all homosexual acts, including those in permanent relationships: 'But if you enter into a permanent relationship, and you are told that too is sin, you cannot repent and be forgiven because the relationship goes on. The Church tells you that you must give it up and if you do you are back all too easily to the round of casual sex...'[10]

Some of the speakers following Higton indicated more support for the position of homosexual clergy, but in the main it is interesting to note that the motion, which called for the removal of practising homosexual clergy from the ministry, was discussed without any evidence about the problems caused by homosexuality among clergy, nor any evidence that such clergy were promiscuous. It did not go unnoticed that part (iii) of the motion would result in the mass removal of ministers. The Bishop of London, for example said, 'It implies that "to remain in office" we who hold office must believe that we are "exemplary in all spheres of morality". I cannot say that – nor can anyone here.'[11] The Reverend Malcolm Johnson said 'I do not know who would be left. There are seven deadly sins, not just one: lust, pride, sloth, gluttony, covetousness, envy, anger. If we have to leave after committing these, the Church will be very short-staffed indeed.'[12]

The particular line of Anthony Higton did not meet with success in Synod although the amendment of the Bishop of Chester, carried by a large majority, stated that Christians should be exemplary in all spheres of morality, including sexual morality, and that homosexual genital acts 'fall short of this ideal'. It did apparently, however, have a very damaging effect on homosexual clergy who have since reported increased isolation, rejection and alienation, and even perceived hostility from their employing body and the secular community.[13] There have been some attempts in Synod to gain acceptance at least for those homosexual clergy in permanent relationships. The Bishop of Stepney, the Right Reverend James Thomson, called for better understanding of the problems of homosexuals, although the Reverend Malcolm Johnson failed in his attempt at the November 1987 meeting to gain acceptance of those in committed and permanent relationships, irrespective of their sexuality. His amendment to Higton's Private Member's Motion asked the Synod to affirm 'the essential of the Biblical message that human love is a reflection of divine love and should be characterised by the permanency and commitment of relationships... the Synod calls for (a) definite encouragement in Christian teaching and example of stability, commitment and permanence in all human relationships; (b) Christian education... in the dangers... of sexual promiscuity...' The amendment was lost by 325 to 46.

The Higton debate changed the homosexual clergy debate because of the descriptive nature of the resolutions passed: before the debate such matters had been discussed in somewhat more general terms. It put a different kind of magnifying glass on the issue; questions and debates became different in nature. It is said to be a characteristic of the bishops that they do not act unless matters are brought to their attention. Such matters are now unavoidable and the general principles more difficult to espouse. At the end of the Higton debate the Reverend David Holloway attempted to get Synod to pass a motion requiring clergy to be 'appropriately disciplined' in cases of sexual immorality (why only sexual immorality?). The motion was, effectively, an attempt to make prescriptions to bishops about what behaviours should require discipline; it was trying to remove autonomy and discretion away from the bishops. In response to a question in Synod on 8 February, which asked whether the diocesan bishops were unwilling to exercise the discipline called for in the Holloway motion, the Archbishop of Canterbury said they had not supported the amendment because the bishops had always exercised such discipline and to vote for it would imply otherwise. Although the motion failed, it is an example of how some people within the Church were, perhaps, attempting to focus issues in a rigorously prescriptive manner without due understanding of the negative consequences of such a strategy. Such a strategy, related again primarily to the issue of homosexuality, is also being pursued in attempts to change the Advisory Council for the Church's Ministry guidelines for selection of candidates (see the section below on the problems of ordination). These moves could be interpreted as an orchestrated attack on a necessarily silent and anonymous group and can at best be described as politically motivated: at worst they represent witch-hunts. As the Archbishop of Canterbury said in the Higton debate, referring to St Paul, 'We are in no position to cast stones. In this earthly tabernacle of Christ's kingdom there are many mansions, and all of them are made of glass.'[14]

While some observers did report softening of the hard attitudes within General Synod[15] a reverse effect may be the consequence of a case which hit General Synod in July 1989. In June 1989 a series of allegations of homosexual and deviant group sexual behaviours were reported in a mass-circulation newspaper against a prominent clergyman who also held an important position in Synod. The allegations in the newspaper were somewhat sensational and obtained by very devious means. Not only did such 'revelations' feed presumptions about homosexuals, however, they also led to two Synod members, Mrs Jill Dann and the Reverend David Holloway, circulating all members with the newspaper article and a letter calling for the clergyman's resignation, which was nothing if not divisive. Whatever the truth of the allegations (the clergyman was said by his bishop not to have committed the acts, only fantasised), the whole sad affair has probably set back the likelihood of considered debate within the Church. It is also likely to result in more unhappiness and psychological distress among homosexual clergy. The attitudes demonstrated by the Church in Synod debates and other public places may well contribute towards more unfortunate cases such as this.

The problems for homosexual candidates at ordination

The traditional teaching of the Church on sexuality is unambiguous: sexual intercourse is permissible only within marriage. This means that in choosing ordination the homosexual is choosing celibacy. Many homosexual clergymen are not celibate and would appeal to higher authorities to defend their position. We have already discussed the difficulties the clergyman has in this regard. There is, however, another matter of central importance that is becoming a significantly more stressful event: the selection procedure for ordination.

The issue of homosexuality is much more to the fore than it used to be and ordinands are quite likely now to be questioned about their sexuality (or at least to have their domestic circumstances scrutinised). There are three strands in the selection process for ministry in the Church of England. The first stage is preselection by the diocese, culminating with the bishop sponsoring appropriate candidates. These candidates then attend selection conferences under the control of the central Church body, the Advisory Council for the Church's Ministry. The final stage is theological college. Candidates who are successful at all stages may then be ordained by the bishop.

At each of these stages there are difficulties for the homosexual candidate. At the first stage he/she may have an unsympathetic bishop and diocesan selectors. At the second, the ACCM guidelines make it more difficult for homosexual candidates. The criteria for selection are embodied in ACCM Occasional Paper No. 12, June 1983. The document is not very explicit about how homosexuality should be weighed in the context of the majority of the criteria, although there is a section on 'Special Considerations' which does discuss homosexuality. Paragraph 7.19 of the criteria on 'Stability' says that emotional and sexual issues are such 'important and significant aspects of personality that they should not be ignored by Selectors... these areas must not be avoided'. It goes on to say that since 'it is the whole person who is offering for ministry, and through whom ministry is effective, there is no information which is not relevant',[16] and at 11.3, 'The Selector is seeking to prompt candidates into disclosing themselves as freely and frankly as possible'. In 'Special Considerations' there is no explicit distinction made between homosexuals in permanent relationships and those who are not. The primary *additional* criterion homosexual clergy would have to satisfy is that of 'pastoral effectiveness'. The Archbishop of Canterbury seems to suggest a relatively more liberal line be taken at ordination. He said in his 27 February 1981 speech at General Synod on homosexuality that 'one of my rule of thumb tests for ordination would be if a man was so obsessive a campaigner on this subject that it made his ministry unavailable to the majority of churchpeople, then I would see no justification in ordaining him'.[17]

Pastoral effectiveness is a general term which the criteria of ACCM do not help to refine or define very much, although they include 'the range of effective relationships a candidate could manage and the effectiveness of a ministry to groups and the wider community as well'[18] and 'Some evidence from the diocese of the local reaction, expectations and acceptability should be made available'[19] and 'selection will therefore take note of relevant points made by the diocese and look for evidence that the generally anticipated level of pastoral effectiveness will not be crucially diminished'.[20] Such criteria, however, are almost certainly going to exclude the homosexual person from ordination because, in many settings, the homosexuality would not be welcomed which could be construed as evidence of reduced pastoral effectiveness. While the criteria do specifically say that the qualities of the whole person should be considered when evaluating effectiveness (for example, the candidate may have particular strengths which are a consequence of his sexuality) it remains difficult for the homosexual, particularly those who are prepared to admit to sexual relationships. Although the ACCM guidelines discuss sexuality as only one area of interest in consideration of pastoral effectiveness, homosexuality is, in many cases, going to be a sufficient condition to stop ordination.

Selection for ordination, therefore, is a major problem for the homosexual ordinand, particularly for the honest and open person: those who wish to be ordained, believe they have the calling of God, believe they can do an excellent job, are committed to lives of caring and Christian faith for the good of others, will significantly reduce their chances of being ordained by mentioning any aspect of their homosexuality. The homosexual person in a permanent relationship which is visible to all is in an even more invidious position.

While there are some liberal bishops and selectors, many ordinands must either lie, waffle or whitewash the issue if they are to be ordained. Some, of course, do not get asked the relevant questions, at least not directly. Those who do, however, are put in a very invidious position which is likely to be stressful itself, and lead to long-term contemplation about their 'lies', forced on them by the traditional perspective. The homosexual candidates must hold some very strong beliefs about their own sexuality and their relationship with God in order to proceed with the possible deceptions. Their ministries and good works, however, are likely to be offset in their own minds by their inability to be open. Some candidates do not seek ordination, even though they believe they are called to it as well as to their relationship with their partner, because it is forbidden. Eric James[21] has suggested that the ACCM statistics concerning ordination are showing the effects of the increased discussion of sexuality in the selection process.

Given these problems, the recent discussions of the ACCM criteria in Synod are likely to make the situation even worse for homosexuals who are called to ministry. For example, in the February and July 1988 General Synods the Chairman of ACCM was asked about the implications of homosexuality for the selection criteria. He was also asked by the Reverend Anthony Higton to 'ensure that all candidates are asked for their views on sexual morality'.[22] In response, the Bishop of Bristol affirmed that the ACCM criteria were clear enough, and that the bishops' selectors were left with the responsibility to decide, using those criteria, if the candidates were suitable to be sponsored for training. When pressed to answer whether the bishops would refuse to recommend for selection candidates who were known to be actively homosexual, the ACCM Chairman refused to answer directly, saying that the responsibility for sponsorship and ordination lay clearly with the diocesan bishops.

This seems to exacerbate the problem for homosexual candidates, increase pressure on them to withhold information, lessen the likelihood of ordaining homosexuals in visible long-term relationships, maximise the ordaining of those more willing to lie and those who are not in permanent relationships. It increases the pressures on ordained homosexuals, it sharpens the focus on sexual, as opposed to general, morality, and it appears negatively reactive, rather than affirming positive values candidates should have for successful ordained ministry.

The definition of homosexuality

It is also probably the case that the Church position on homosexuality would vary somewhat depending upon what was deemed to count as homosexuality: thinking about it, disposition, or action. It would not be as bad to have homosexual thoughts as long as nothing is done about them in practice – as long as there was no sex. It has been clear in my interactions with the Church that a good number of the bishops believe that most homosexual clergy are not practising homosexuals: they do not do anything about their sexual drives and inclinations. It has been equally clear in my researches with the clergy that many are not celibate. The Gloucester Report Working Party obviously realised this too when it suggested that 'to declare that homosexuals may not in any circumstances give physical expression to their erotic love is unduly to circumscribe the area of responsible choice... in the light of some of the evidence we have received we do not think it possible to deny that there are circumstances in which individuals may justifiably choose to enter into a homosexual relationship with the hope of enjoying a companionship and sexual love similar to that which is to be found in marriage',[23] although the Report did then conclude that a priest living in sexual union with another man should offer his resignation.

As Eric James has discussed in his document *Homosexuality and a Pastoral Church* there are many important definitional difficulties with the use of the term 'homosexual'. A working definition such as 'a preference for sexual relations with one's own sex' does not clarify the situation in a helpful way because, he claims:

a) that preference is not always exclusive
b) it would appear to belong to most people for some part of their life
c) the evidence is that there is more than one cause for such a preference
d) there is still a great deal of uncertainty about the origins of such a preference; so that it may be more accurate to speak of 'homosexualities' – plural.[24]

In the 27 February 1981 debate on the Gloucester Report, the Archbishop of Canterbury, who said he saw homosexuality as 'neither a sin nor as sickness but as handicap',[25] makes the distinction between the use of the term 'homosexual' as a noun (people) and as an adjective (acts) and suggested that 'the danger was there of tyrannically imposing the categories heterosexual, homosexual, on a range of relationships and feelings which cannot be categorised in such a banal and crude way'.[26] It is perhaps better to confine the use of the term to refer to *behaviour* which includes homosexual genital activity. In addition, to exclude the category of homosexual activity which may occur as a developmental phase in youth, we should only refer to genital acts which occur after 'youth' is over. This will not, of course, have implications for clergy since, as we have seen, the age profile of stipendiary clergy is not a young one. The study reported here also suggests that homosexuality among clergy is more common than the Church has previously admitted publicly.

What can be done?

Solutions will not come easily or quickly, nor will they come without the expense of some compromise. It is all too easy for the homosexual clergy to project blame on the Church, but society obviously contributes to the difficult position for them too. Equally, however, it is all too easy for the Church to absolve itself of responsibility and to criticise the clergy for their sexuality and say it is against the teachings of the Church. The Church undoubtedly has an easy time publicly if it takes this position since a proportion of the lay society would agree with it. It is not, however, the moral duty of the Church to accept easy answers! What is required are bold and just solutions which come to grips with the complex truth and thus with the problem which undoubtedly exists for a large number of people whether they are on Church of England stipends or not. The Church cannot have a reputation for caring for its clergy and ignore the stress of its homosexual clergy. But this will involve confronting the issue of sexuality generally and not evading the issues.

The position is not easy for all that. The immediate problem is how the stressed clergy can be helped. This brief chapter considers some possible solutions. Some of these would require the Church to engage in open discussion on the issue of sexuality – something that it has not found easy to do in the past. Some of the suggestions simply involve the Church accepting that something should be done to alleviate the very difficult circumstances homosexual clergy find themselves in: these problems will not go away if ignored – on the contrary. The Church will not simply want to reflect the current prejudices of society and some of the suggestions will, therefore, involve the Church taking a lead in society over the issue of sexuality. Some of the suggestions must be acted on for the sake of the Church's reputation as a good employer, as well as for the sake of its employees. A prior step towards any solution is that the Church begin to defuse the atmosphere of mistrust and suspicion which the evidence reveals currently exists between those who are employed and those with responsibilities as employers.

Suggested ways forward

1. **Promotion of widespread debate**. The subject of stress, independent of the issue of homosexuality, should not be left to the bishops alone. It needs to be discussed, in all its aspects as they affect the Church, in the General Synod, in Deanery Synods, in Parish Councils, among ordinary clergy, etc., and at all levels. For genuine discussion to take place this must be done in groups in which mutual trust has been established.

2. **Study of sexuality**. It has been clear from the previous chapters that the Church could usefully seek greater understanding of the issues surrounding human sexuality. Some of these issues have surfaced in this book. As a first step it is to be hoped that the Church will broadly accept the research findings presented in this book in good faith. This research has, however, left many questions unanswered. What is needed, surely, is for the Church to initiate a proper study of sexuality. Such a study should not be based on a campaigning ethic but be concerned with real human and theological enquiry. A study of sexuality would inform the bishops about the pastoral needs in two ways. It would, of course, educate them more about sexuality in general, and inevitably about their own sexuality in particular. And if the bishops had a better understanding of the issues they might well be more open about the subject of homosexuality among clergy, and be better equipped to discuss the ethical and practical ramifications.

One area which requires careful and unprejudiced research is in the theology, psychology and sociology of *representative* priesthood as it affects homosexual clergy in theory and practice.

It is maintained by many that the basis of priesthood is *humanity* rather than simply *maleness*. Part of the debate about the ordination of women concerns the question whether a woman – single or married – can represent humanity. Many presuppose that a woman cannot do this. It is often much more a matter of 'gut feeling' than theology or research. Similarly, with the question of whether or not only a celibate male and/or only a heterosexual male can be representative in this way. There are gut feelings in the preference for celibates but these preferences may well result from guilt over sex. There are also gut feelings in the rejection of the possibility of homosexual 'representativeness'.

Of course, homosexuals are not the norm in society, so that there is the problem of a minority being representative. But celibates have always been only a minority too and no one says that they cannot be representative priests.

Sometimes, the 'representative' question is discussed under the subject of *'focal'* people: priests as those who focus. Sometimes the representative question is discussed under the subject of priests as 'sacraments'. Austin Farrer used to call priests 'walking sacraments' – particular people who are sacramental of all humanity. Is this 'gut feeling' or is there valid theology behind the rejection? The Church has a duty to clarify this to homosexual ordinands who believe they have a vocation, to the Church as a whole, and to the world. The attitude of the Episcopal Church (Anglican) in the Diocese of San Francisco to homosexual clergy is considerably different from the Church of England – so there really appears to be something that needs to be discussed and researched in England.

It goes without saying that many local churches will need to be educated about sexuality if they are to accept a homosexual priest as their representative. This is only to face facts – the facts that are responsible for much of the stress of homosexual clergy.

3. **The need to redefine the Church structure with respect to care, control and counsel**. The present structure of the Church creates severe problems for both clergy and Church because it seems to vest care, control and counsel overwhelmingly at one level (the bishop). The result is an authority–pastoral sharing problem. The Church has a very structured hierarchy (consider, for example, the hierarchy of titles and ways to address the different Church personnel). This very secular structure of authority, however, poses as an entirely sacred one, creating problems for clergy who have personal difficulties and clergy who may require advice or counsel. This problem can be demonstrated by an example at the selection stage of candidates, as well as at the much later stage of caring for the individual ordained clergyman.

To appoint a person, you need to know him. To allow yourself to be known understandably requires a considerable act of trust. If you allow yourself to be 'shepherded' – to be known in order to be cared for, supported and healed – that knowledge may be taken down and used in evidence against you by those who have the responsibility of advising whoever has the ultimate responsibility of appointing or not appointing you: you will feel, and may in fact be, betrayed. Yet those with the appointing power are bound to take all their knowledge of you into account.

Within the Church's episcopal system of unified care, appointment and deployment through the person of the bishop there is a dilemma which is seldom faced, let alone resolved, and which relates not least to the present problem of the homosexual priest. 'You can tell me all: I am your Shepherd, Bishop and Friend... but now I know, I cannot possibly appoint you.' In fact the problem is even more complex. May the bishop share what he knows *personally* with the *corporate bodies* now involved in appointments – bishop's staff meeting, patronage boards, church wardens, etc.? There are complex questions here of mutual care and trust, and of confidentiality, of difference of principle and belief within corporate bodies, of authority and power – but, not least, also of human weakness and corruption within the Church.

It is urgent that these matters, in relation particularly to homosexual clergy, are faced.

4. **Recognition and development of an ethic for those in committed same-sex relationships**. Not all practising homosexual clergy are in stable, committed, long-term relationships, although 25 per cent of the study sample were. It is suggested that current policy of the Church establishment does not encourage faithfulness and commitment between same-sex partners and may, indeed, be directly responsible for some promiscuity that occurs, as well as the strain it places on some individuals. It is surely now necessary for the Church to change policy. Evidence shows that committed relationships provide partners with a protective buffer from stress and illness. From all the evidence presented in this book it seems critical that the Church should, as a matter of policy, distinguish between faithful and committed same-sex relationships and those of a more temporary nature. What is needed surely is a positive ethic for committed and stable homosexual relationships analogous to heterosexual marriage. The Church needs to encourage a lifelong commitment between homosexual partners in much the same way it does between heterosexual partners. What form such 'recognition' could take is more difficult. Bishop Spong of the Episcopal Church in the USA has suggested that homosexual couples should be offered some form of church service, to formalise the commitment. He writes: 'I call upon the churches of this land to revive a concept of betrothal and to install it as a valid option and sign of a serious commitment, even though it falls short of the legal status of marriage'.[27] Such a suggestion may seem somewhat radical. But it is surely for the Church to consider how it may provide for homosexuals that 'mutual society, help, and comfort, that the one ought to have of the other, both in prosperity and adversity'.[28]

5. **Establish a comprehensive support group network**. In many

dioceses there are pastoral counselling councils/groups which are concerned with the pastoral needs of all clergy. Some homosexual clergy also belong to special support networks. Neither of these has a proper formalised structure (indeed, the latter has to operate in a very clandestine manner). It has been clear from the research in this book that loneliness and isolation can be major stressors for clergy. Formal recognition of the need for support groups spread across the whole country, in both rural and urban areas, would serve to reduce the feelings of isolation and provide a buffer for stress. Only a small amount of money would be required to set up such networks. The Church would, however, have to acknowledge that there was such a need. In addition, it would also have to accept that there does not exist sufficient trust between homosexual clergy and the Church for the latter to organise it. A framework for the solution of some of these dilemmas would be to establish an independent support service for all clergy.

6. **The formation of an independent and confidential advisory and counselling service**. What is required is a solution which can be offered by the Church in its function as a caring employer, but which does not compromise the position of the clergy on significant issues (such as homosexuality). One obvious option is for the Church of England to set up an independent and confidential employee advisory and counselling programme for all clergy and their families. The service should not only be independent of the Church of England, but also of the clergy support groups that exist for homosexual clergy, and the various organisations which exist to help them. Such programmes have been employed to great effect in industry and commerce and the author has been influential in designing and setting up what is probably the archetypal one in the UK, known as EAR.[29]

The objective would be to provide an accessible and confidential source of advice and counselling for *all* clergy of the Church of England. The main guiding principles of the programme would be:

Independence: Many clergy (whatever their sexuality, but especially homosexual clergy) would not take certain issues and problems to a service unless it was organised to be totally independent of the Church of England. There would be no reason for the service to be run by those who were currently employed by the Church of England and its independence would be better secured if this was not the case. The service would have to be designed specifically for the Church, however, since the nature of the problems raised would be likely to be different from those raised by other working populations.

Availability: Because of the geographic spread of clergy throughout England the initial contact would be made via a telephone number to counsellors who could be located anywhere in the country. Provision could be made outside office hours with little difficulty, although a 9–5 provision would seem adequate initially. If clergy needed to see a counsellor in person they could either visit the central offices or arrange to be visited.

Wide scope: The service would aim to provide help and advice with any problem, personal or work related, to any clergyman or woman or their family (including partners). The service would provide advice and counselling, but would draw on a wide variety of specialist areas including medicine and psychology, law, finance and consumer affairs. The cost of initial professional services would be free, but if more than guidance was required they would be referred to an appropriate resource and pay as normal.

Voluntary and free: The service should be free and entirely voluntary.

The philosophy of such a service would have to be to help people to help themselves by providing either information, counselling, or referral. The caller could also remain completely anonymous (which would be a considerable advantage for some homosexual clergy).

The service would have a number of potential benefits for all clergy, not just homosexual clergy. It has been found that such provisions in industry can improve morale, result in more efficient work, greater commitment and better organisational functioning. An important benefit is that the service is in a unique position to be able to identify particular 'hot spots', and areas of policy or procedure which could be improved or initiated. Such information could be reported to the Church without identifying specific individuals. The service would benefit all Church of England employees and would promote the view that it was a caring employer. Certainly something along these lines is needed.

Notes

1. James, 1988.
2. Paragraph 170 of The Gloucester Report.
3. Paragraph 261 of The Gloucester Report.
4. Paragraph 221 of The Gloucester Report.
5. Paragraph 171 of The Gloucester Report.
6. Report on Proceedings of General Synod, 1981, pp. 434–5.
7. James, 1988, pp. 5–6.
8. Report on Proceedings, 1988, vol. 18, no. 3, p. 913.
9. *Ibid.*, p. 915.
10. *Ibid.*, p. 940.
11. *Ibid.*, p. 920.
12. *Ibid.*, p. 923.
13. For example, Leech, 1988.
14. Report on Proceedings, 1988, vol. 18, no. 3, p. 926.
15. For example, Longley, 1989.
16. ACCM Occasional Paper no. 12, June 1983, Paragraph 11.2.
17. Report on Proceedings, 1981, p. 414.
18. ACCM Occasional Paper no. 12, June 1983, Paragraph 12.26.
19. *Ibid.*, Paragraph 12.27.
20. *Ibid.*, Paragraph 12.28.
21. James, 1988.
22. Report on Proceedings, 1988, p. 30.
23. Paragraph 168 of The Gloucester Report.
24. James, 1988, pp. 11–12.
25. Report on Proceedings, 1981, p. 414.
26. Report on Proceedings, 1981, p. 413.
27. Spong, 1990, chapter 12, 'Betrothal: an idea whose time has come', p. 177.
28. 1928 Prayer Book.
29. Fletcher and Hall, 1984.

References

ACCM Occasional Paper No. 12 (1983) *Selection for Ministry: a report on criteria.* June 1983.

Ader, R. and Cohen, N. (1985) CNS–immune system interactions: conditioning phenomena. *The Behavioural and Brain Sciences*, **8**, 379–94.

Alfredsson, L., Karasek, R. A. and Theorell, T. (1982) Myocardial infarction risk and psychosocial environment – an analysis of the male Swedish working force. *Social Science and Medicine*, **16**, 463–7.

Babuscio, J. (1988) *We Speak for Ourselves: the experiences of gay men and lesbian women.* SPCK: London, revised edition.

Bailey, D. S. (1955) *Homosexuality and the Western Christian Tradition.* Longman: London.

Berkman, L. F. and Syme, S. L. (1979) Social networks, host resistance, and mortality: a nine-year follow-up study of Alameda County residents. *American Journal of Epidemiology*, **109**(2), 186–204.

Blackmon, R. A. (1984) *The hazards of ministry.* Unpublished PhD thesis, Fuller Theological Seminary, Pasadena, CA.

Booth-Kewley, S. and Friedman, H. S. (1987) Psychological predictors of heart disease: a quantitative review. *Psychological Bulletin*, **101**, 343–62.

Boswell, J. (1981) *Christianity, Social Tolerance and Homosexuality.* University of Chicago Press.

Cecchi, R. L. (1984) Stress: prodrome to immune deficiency. *Annals of the New York Academy of Sciences*, **437**, 286–9.

Church of England Year Book (1988) Church House Publishing: London, 104th edition.

Church of England Year Book (1989) Church House Publishing: London, 105th edition.

Crown, S. and Crisp, A. H. (1979) *Manual of the Crown–Crisp Experiential Index*. Hodder and Stoughton: London.

Daniel, S. P. and Rogers, M. L. (1981) Burnout and the pastorate: A critical review with implications for pastors. *Journal of Psychology and Theology*, **9**(3), 232–49.

Dewe, P. J. (1987) New Zealand ministers of religion: identifiying sources of stress and coping processes. *Work and Stress*, **1**(4), 351–64.

Doohan, H. (1982) Burnout: A critical issue for the 1980s. *Journal of Religion and Health*, **21**(4), 352–8.

Dunn, R. (1965) Personality patterns among religious personnel: a review. *The Catholic Psychological Record*, **3**(2), 125–37.

Ellis, L., Ames, M. A., Peckham, W. and Burke, D. (1988) Sexual orientation of human offspring may be altered by severe maternal stress during pregnancy. *Journal of Sex Research*, **25**(1), 152–7.

Eysenck, H. J. (1988) Personality, stress and cancer: prediction and prophylaxis. *British Journal of Medical Psychology*, **61**(1), 57–76.

Fay, R. E., Turner, C. F., Klassen, A. D. and Gagnon, J. H. (1989) Prevalence and patterns of same-gender sexual contact among men. *Science*, **243**, 338–48.

Fletcher, B. (C.) (1988a) The epidemiology of occupational stress. In C. L. Cooper and R. L. Payne (eds) *Causes, Coping and Consequences of Stress at Work*. J. Wiley and Sons: London.

Fletcher, B. (C.) (1988b) Occupation, marriage and disease-specific mortality concordance. *Social Science and Medicine*, **27**(6), 615–22.

Fletcher, B. (C.) (1990) *The Cultural Audit: an individual and organisational investigation*. PSI Pub.

Fletcher, B. (C.) *Work, Stress, Disease and Life Expectancy*. J. Wiley and Sons: Chichester.

Fletcher, B. (C.) and Hall, J. (1984) Coping with personal problems at work. *Personnel Management*, February, 30–3.

Fletcher, B. (C.) and MacPherson, D. A. J. (1989) Stressors and strains in Church of England parochial clergy. Presented to the British Psychological Society, London.

Fletcher, B. (C.) and Morris, D. (1989) A comparison of 'Knowledge Boys' and London licensed taxi drivers: a causal interpretation of the role of taxi driving in psychological ill-health. *Third European Conference on Health Psychology: Life Styles and Health,* Utrecht, 1989.

Fletcher, B. (C.) and Payne, R. L. (1980a) Stress at work: A review and theoretical framework. Part 1. *Personnel Review,* **9**(1), 19–29.

Fletcher, B. (C.). and Payne, R.L. (1980b) Stress at work: A review and theoretical framework. Part 2. *Personnel Review,* **9**(2), 4–8.

Fletcher, B. (C.) and Payne, R. L. (1982) Levels of reported stressors and strains amongst schoolteachers: some UK data. *Educational Review,* **34**, 267–8.

Fletcher, B. (C.) and Payne, R. L. (1983) Job demands, supports, and constraints as predictors of psychological strain among schoolteachers. *Journal of Vocational Behaviour,* **22**, 136–47.

Folkman, S. (1984) Personal control and stress and coping processes: a theoretical analysis. *Personality and Social Psychology,* **46**(4), 839–52.

Forman, D. and Chivers, C. (1989) Sexual behaviour of young and middle-aged men in England and Wales. *British Medical Journal,* **298**, 1137–42.

Frankenhaeuser, M. (1975) Sympathetic–adrenomedullary activity, behaviour and the psychosocial environment. In P. H. Venables and M. J. Christie (eds) *Research in Psychophysiology.* John Wiley: New York.

Geis, S. B., Fuller, R. L. and Rush, J. (1986) Lovers of AIDS victims: psychological stresses and counselling needs. *Death Studies,* **10**(1), 43–53.

Goodwin, J. S., Hunt, W. C., Key, C. R. and Samet, J.M. (1987) The effect of marital status on stage, treatment, and survival of cancer patients. *Journal of the American Medical Association,* **258**(21), 3125–30.

Greer, S., Morris, T. and Pettingdale, K. W. (1979) Psychological response to breast cancer: effect on outcome. *Lancet,* **2**, 785–7.

Hall, R. C. W. and Gardner, E. R. (1979) The professional burnout syndrome. *Psychiatric Opinion,* **16**(4), 12–17.

Holme, I., Helgeland, A., Hjerman, I., Leren, P. and Lund-Larsen, P. G. (1977) Coronary risk factors in various occupational groups: the Oslo study. *British Journal of Preventative and Social Medicine,* **31**, 96–100.

Homosexual Relationships: a contribution to discussion (The Gloucester

Report)(1979). CIO Publishing, Church House: London.

James, E. (1988) *Homosexuality and a Pastoral Church: a plea for study and discussion*. Christian Action: London.

Karasek, R. A. (1979) Job demands, job decision latitude and mental strain: implications for job design. *Administrative Science Quarterly*, **24**, 285–308.

Karasek, R. A., Russell, R. S. and Theorell, T. (1982) Physiology of stress and regeneration in job related cardiovascular illness. *Journal of Human Stress*, **8**(1), 29–42.

Karasek, R. A., Theorell, T. G. T., Schwartz, J., Pieper, C. and Alfredsson, L. (1982) Job, psychological factors and coronary heart disease. *Advanced Cardiology*, **29**, 62–7.

Kasl, S. V. (1978) Epidemiological contributions to the study of work stress. In C. L. Cooper and R. L. Payne (eds) *Stress at Work*. John Wiley and Sons: New York.

Kennedy, S., Kiecolt-Glaser, J. K. and Glaser, R. (1988) Immunological consequences of acute and chronic stressors: mediating role of interpersonal relationships. *British Journal of Medical Psychology*, **61**(1), 77–86.

Kiecolt-Glaser, J. K., Fisher, L., Ogrocki, P., Stout, J. C., Speicher, C. E. and Glaser, R. (1987) Marital quality, marital disruption and immune function. *Psychosomatic Medicine*, **49,** 13–34.

Kinsey, A. C., Pomeroy, W. B. and Martin, C. E. (1949) *Sexual Behaviour in the Human Male*. W. B. Saunders Co: Philadelphia and London.

Krantz, D. S., Arabian, J. M., Davia, J. E. and Parker, J. S. (1982) Type A behaviour and coronary bypass surgery: intraoperative blood pressure and perioperative complications. *Psychosomatic Medicine*, **44**(3), 273–84.

Lauer, R. H. (1973) Organisational punishment: punitive relations in a voluntary association. *Human Relations*, **26**(2) 189–202.

Lazarus, R. S. (1966) *Psychological Stress and the Coping Process*. McGraw-Hill: New York.

Leech, K. (1988) Crisis for gays in the Church of England. *The Christian Century*, 678–9.

Longley, C. (1989) Homosexuality battle at an end. *The Times* (London), 4 February.

MacDonald, G. (1980) Dear church, I quit. *Christianity Today*, 27 June, 17–21.

MacPherson, D. A. J. (1989) *Occupational stress amongst parochial clergy in the Church of England*. MSc thesis, Hatfield Polytechnic.

Martin, J. L. (1988) Psychological consequences of AIDS-related bereavement among gay men. *Journal of Consulting and Clinical Psychology*, **56**(6), 856–62.

Maslach, C. (1978) Job burnout: How people cope. *Public Welfare*, **36**, 56–8.

Maslach, C. (1982) *Burnout: the cost of caring*. Prentice-Hall: Englewood Cliffs, NJ.

OPCS (1986) *Occupational Mortality 1979–80, 1982–3: Decennial supplement*, Part I, Commentary, Part II, Microfiche tables. Series DS no. 6, HMSO: London.

Payne, R. L. (1979) Demands, supports, constraints and psychological health. In C. J. Mackay and T. Cox (eds) *Responses to Stress: occupational aspects*. International Publishing Corporation: London.

Payne, R. L. and Jones, J. G. (1987) Measurement and methodological issues in social support. In S. V. Kasl and C. L. Cooper, *Stress and Health: issues in research methodology*. J. Wiley and Sons: Chichester.

Platt, N. V. and Moos, D. M. (1976) Self-perceptive dispositions of Episcopal clergy wives. *Journal of Religion and Health*, **15**(3), 191–209.

Ragland, D. R. and Brand, R. J. (1988a) Coronary heart disease mortality in the Western Collaborative Group Study: follow-up experience of 22 years. *American Journal of Epidemiology*, **127**(3), 462–75.

Ragland, D. R. and Brand, R. J. (1988b) Type A behaviour and mortality from coronary heart disease. *The New England Journal of Medicine*, **318**(2), 65–9.

Rayburn, C. A., Richmond, L. J. and Rogers, L. (1986) Men, women, and religion: stress within leadership roles. *Journal of Clinical Psychology*, **42**(3), 540–6.

Rich, C. L., Fowler, R. C., Young, D. and Blenkush, M. (1986) San Diego suicide study: comparison of gay to straight males. *Suicide and Life Threatening Behaviour*, **64**(4), 448–57.

Richmond, L. J., Rayburn, C. and Rogers, L. (1985) Clergymen, clergywomen, and their spouses: stress in professional religious families. Special issue: family–career linkages. *Journal of Career Development*, **12**(1), 81–6.

Rosser, B. S. and Ross, M. W. (1988) Perceived emotional and life change impact of AIDS on homosexual men in two countries. *Psychology of Health*, **2**(4), 301–17.

Rozanski, A., Bairey, N., Krantz, D. S. *et al.* (1988) Mental stress and the induction of silent myocardial ischemia in patients with coronary artery disease. *The New England Journal of Medicine*, **318**(16), 1005–12.

Samy, E. A. (1988) Experience of stress among Catholic Diocesan priests of Tamil Nadu, India. *Dissertations Abstracts International*, **48**(12-A), 3053–4.

Schmale, A. H. and Iker, H. P. (1966) The affect of hopelessness and the development of cancer. *Journal of Psychosomatic Medicine*, **28**, 714–21.

Selye, H. (1976) *The Stress of Life*. McGraw-Hill: New York.

Smith, G. R. and MacDaniel, S. M. (1983) Psychologically mediated effect on the delayed hypersensitivity reaction to tuberculin in humans. *Psychosomatic Medicine*, **45**, 65–70.

Spong, J. S. (1990) *Living in Sin: a bishop rethinks human sexuality*. Harper and Row: San Francisco.

Stone, F. W. (1985) *Measures to reduce stress at work*. Unpublished PhD thesis. University of Aston in Birmingham.

Swogger, G. (1981) Toward understanding stress: a map of the territory. *Journal of Social Health*, **51**, 29–33.

Thomas, C. B., Duszynski, K. R. and Shaffer, J. W. (1979) Family attitudes reported in youth as potential predictors of cancer. *Psychosomatic Medicine*, **41**, 287–302.

Trujillo, R. (1985) Job stress and strain in the parish ministry. *Dissertations Abstracts International*, **45**(12-B, Pt 1), 3965–6.

Vachon, M. L. (1986) Myths and realities in palliative/hospice care. Special issue: Nursing in hospice and terminal care: research and practice. *Hospice Journal*, **2**(1), 63–79.

Warner, J. and Carter, J. D. (1984) Loneliness, marital adjustment and burnout in pastoral and lay persons. *Journal of Psychology and Theology*, **12**(2), 125–31.

Warr, P. (1987) *Work, Unemployment and Mental Health*. Oxford University Press: Oxford.